England's History

ENGLAND'S GLORY

(1966 and all that . . .)

Dave Hill

PAN BOOKS

First published 1996 by Pan Books

an imprint of Macmillan Publishers Ltd
25 Eccleston Place, London SW1W 9NF
and Basingstoke

Associated companies throughout the world

ISBN 0 330 34743 8

1 3 5 7 9 8 6 4 2

A CIP catalogue record for this book is available from
the British Library

Phototypeset by Intype London Ltd
Printed by Mackays of Chatham PLC, Chatham, Kent

For Sheila, the lovely left-footer
For Laura, Frankie and Nat, in my first team for ever
For Dolores Moira Rose, new star in the squad

Contents

Pre-Match

Sunday, 28 May 1995

BUTLIN'S HOLIDAY World, Bognor Regis, a cavalcade
of down-market southern English kitsch. It's a wet
Sunday morning but the day may yet be saved by today's
special guest at the Cockney Pride theme pub as adver-
tised in the Entertainments Programme: '1.45 pm –
Question and Answer Session with Geoff Hurst'.

I want to be there, but for slightly ignoble reasons.
One is a rather mischievous interest in the ways Mr
Hurst makes his living. I know he has a proper job with
a south Essex vehicle insurance firm, and that one of
his colleagues is a Mr Peters (who I'm quite interested
in too). But it's the bits Mr Hurst does on the side that
intrigue. For instance, when I went to Upton Park to
watch West Ham United recently he appeared in the
match programme advertising a brand of double-glazed
mock-Tudor windows. Then there was the television
programme I'd worked on in which Mr Hurst agreed
to appear for a fee of £300. How much, I wonder to
myself, does he get for his half-hour stint in the Cockney
Pride?

Of course, I won't ask him that when he settles on
to his bar stool. And really, I'm not being sniffy. The

country is full of people trading on past glory and, unlike most of them, Mr Hurst did something to deserve it. Nor will I be brave enough to put the question I really want to know the answer to which is: are you sick of being asked about the 1966 World Cup and all matters relating to it? Such as how do you get on with Jimmy Greaves? How did you feel when Bobby Moore died? And, most persistent of all, come on now, Geoff, be honest – did it cross the line?

But there is a more honourable reason for my fascination too. On 30 July 1966 when I was eight years old Mr Hurst did something unique and very public which enthralled me, changed my life in a way, and remains imprinted on the folk memories of millions of fellow Englishmen and Englishwomen too. One measure of the longevity of these folk memories is the amount of trivia they retain: anecdotes about Russian linesmen and dogs called Pickles and, of course, a list of names which rolls off the most unlikely tongues with quite astonishing ease: Banks, Cohen, Wilson, Stiles, Charlton J., Moore (captain), Ball, Hunt, Charlton R., Hurst, Peters.

But another measure has a more elusive nature and is all muddled up with what are often claimed to be the essential qualities of the English people: honesty, phlegmatism, guts, endurance, decency, dignity, resourcefulness under pressure. England is replete with stories about itself dominated by such traits, and Mr Hurst is a character in one of the most popular of all. Not the leading character, not even a defining one. But his role in the legend is decisive and even the tawdriest setting cannot dim its beauty. Not even a wet day in Bognor.

But this day is doomed to be a bad one. Just before noon, three blokes in their forties gather round the door of the Cockney Pride. A handwritten note has been taped to the bolted doors. The ink has been smeared by the drizzle, but the message has survived: 'Geoff Hurst Cancelled Due to Illness.'

'Oh,' says the first bloke, disappointed. 'I was looking forward to that.'

'Me too,' says the second.

The third looks rather puzzled. 'Who's Geoff Hurst then?' he enquires.

The first two look at each other, then look at the third, aghast. Can this man be serious? Where has he been for the last thirty years?

One

Sunday, 19 June 1966

A SUMMER'S AFTERNOON in rural Shropshire and twenty-seven weary Englishmen make their way towards a converted country house to inspect their bruises and shower their sweat away. They are young men, none much more than thirty, some barely out of their teens, all of them lean and fit, all of them urban and plebeian. Their blue-collar accents clash with the rural setting: geordie, cockney, scouse, small-town Lancashire and more. Turn the clock back twenty years and the same sorts of young men would have been queuing for demob suits. Turn it back fifty and similar combinations would have been huddled fearfully in trenches somewhere in France. But this is 1966 and Englishmen like these have better lives to lead.

These young men have done well for themselves, much better than their dads. Although lawyers and accountants earn more, they are making fifty, sixty, seventy quid a week and upwards. It's a decent wage. And they've got something else going for them: all have travelled a long way down a narrow road to fame and glory. Many thousands envy and admire them. And they have the good luck to love their work. They are, by and large, the sons of steelworkers and pitmen and the like, and some, the older ones, have even done such jobs themselves. All of them appreciate that a career in football beats working for a living by miles.

On this day, though, they know better than ever that what they're part of is more than a game. Many are much quieter than they've been for most of the previous fortnight. All of them know that heartache is heading the way of five of them, and that it will be delivered by another man who's walking with the group, also fit but in his mid-forties, with a wide, bland face, a heavy brow and greying, thinning hair. Some of the young men – maybe a dozen or so – feel safe enough from the older man's unwanted attentions. But the rest watch him edgily from the corners of their eyes, thinking, Please don't come near me, Alf, please, please, please.

Too bad. Alf Ramsey is the England team manager and it is three weeks before the start of the eighth World Cup competition. Only twenty-two of those he's invited for a fortnight's intensive training in the handsome grounds of Lilleshall can be named in his squad for the biggest sporting event ever seen in this country. The twenty-seven have been closeted together like squaddies in a barracks, training together, eating, bathing and playing together, watching the occasional movie, staying away from the booze. They've been examined by Dr Alan Bass, the Football Association's medical director, been put through their paces by Wilf McGuinness, an extra, temporary coach brought in from Manchester United, and drilled to exhaustion by Les Cocker, a hard little trainer from Leeds. Ramsey has participated in all this, encouraged and supervised. But he's also stepped back, comparing notes with Harold Shepherdson from Middlesbrough, his chief trainer and right-hand man. Everyone wishes they knew what he was thinking. Nobody really does. That's how it is with Alf.

The luckless five will just have to live with it. For the rest though, especially the ones who are holding their breath, it will be a time for private exaltation – private, out of deference for the feelings of the crushed quintet. And a few days later they'll all be back together – happy lads together – on a jet aircraft heading for warm-up matches in Scandinavia and Poland before the real business begins back home in the birthplace of the greatest game. The nation is all expectation, and why not? We invented football, after all.

The players will be the principal performers. But the most searching spotlight is already on Ramsey. He doesn't care for the glare, but he's stuck with it. The cult of the manager is growing. The men on the bench are increasingly seen as the alchemists, the psychologists, the masterminds behind the bodies that take the field. But in Ramsey's case it is also because he has taken exceptional power unto himself. No previous England manager has enjoyed such autonomy. For most of the postwar years (and before) line-ups for internationals have been selected by a Football Association committee of gentlemen in suits. Ramsey's long-standing predecessor, Walter Winterbottom, conducted even the 1962 World Cup campaign in Chile under a vestige of its patrician and unwanted influence. But Ramsey's appointment the following year marked an overdue rec-

ognition of a more profound transition in the way football people went about their trade.

Winterbottom managed from the sidelines, sometimes in a suit and tie. But he was not a fuddy-duddy.
A half-back with Manchester United in the late Thirties,
he left the game to become a lecturer in PE, organized
training for the Air Ministry during the war, and
returned as a coaching pioneer, a champion of the
appliance of soccer science. Erecting a blackboard in
front of working-class wizards and sturdy stoppers
formed from the salt of the earth caused culture clashes
at first. But Winterbottom's diagrams mapped the direction of change. Method made its way into a sport of
spontaneous urges, and by the time he stepped down
football was a profession as well as a recreation.

Alf Ramsey is a professional from socks to cerebel-
lum. He is obsessed with football. It isn't just skills and
individuals he considers with such restless fascination,
but entire team formations, whole systems of play. He
never stops: sit Alf at a dinner table and he's got the
condiments marking zonally. Tirelessly he seeks ways
to make a team add up to something more formidable
than simply the sum of its individual parts. Ramsey is
concerned with divining optimum combinations of
talent and with the eradication of error, and he pursues
these objectives his own way, brooking no interference
at all. In Ramsey's mind the biggest threat of failure
seems to lie in heeding other people telling him what to
do. He's accepted the England job on the condition that
this is something he'll never have to endure.

But while he has forced those terms on his

employers, he can't do the same to the public or the press. And they have long decided that he's a strange one, cautious and remote. Ramsey wears a tracksuit with his players. But he cuts an old-fashioned public figure. He talks a bit posh. Though born and raised in Dagenham, an overspill town on London's eastern apron, he has taken elocution lessons to reacquaint his vowels with his aitches and restart his glottal stop. The result is immensely unnatural, but it isn't just the sound of Ramsey's words that grates, it is also their selection. Acquired verbal tics litter his pronouncements, a 'most certainly' here, an 'in respect of' there. His affected syntax and enunciation have become his trademark in the eyes and ears of those increasing millions who encounter him on television, but rather than enhancing his powers of communication, they make his style pedantic and his meaning opaque. His face betrays not even the ghost of an emotion. His mouth moves with the reluctance of a letterbox's slot and demonstrates a similar reluctance to divulge what lies within.

This linguistic stiltedness and apparent deference to imagined betters is sharply at odds with the new breed of populist football managers, living folk legends seen as being blessed with almost mystical gifts. At Manchester United, Matt Busby is a sacred soccer sage, sire of the Busby Babes and a survivor of the aircrash in Munich in 1958 in which so many of them perished. At Liverpool, the Ayrshireman Bill Shankly has built a championship-winning team almost uncannily in the image of both his and his adopted city's wit, grit and know-how. Another, brasher Scot, Tommy Docherty, is talking up his Chelsea side as the charmers of the metropolis. From the outside, compared with these rough-cut diamonds, Ramsey can resemble a relic from a prissy English past.

In the tumultuous new England of seaside scooter riots, Twiggy and the Rolling Stones, he seems a man out of time. The demotic is becoming desirable, forelocks are ceasing to be touched. Homosexual entrepreneurs are replacing gentlemen's outfitters with boutiques. Philip Larkin's poem jokes that 'sexual intercourse began in 1963 ... between the end of the *Chatterley* ban and the Beatles' first LP'. In Larkin's terms Alf Ramsey is still a virgin. But then the football world as a whole remains intact to a great degree. Yes, it knows the frisson of the end of the maximum wage and, yes, it has felt the thrill of enhanced contractual freedom. But this permissiveness is still quite novel and its boundaries are still being tested. At some clubs the odd board member continues to address players by their surnames. And while a few footballers have judged beauty contests, none have thrilled the paparazzi by stepping out under the bright lights with the more successful contestants. Their motor cars are more up-market, but their haircuts are still short. George Best, the fabulous footballer from Belfast, is already destroying defences. George Best, the sexpot superstar, is only just being dreamed up.

So Ramsey and his men are touched by the emerging mood, but do not represent it. They have been formed by the more seasoned England of clock cards, class barriers and Churchillian convictions and that mould has not been broken yet. In football terms, though, they are completely up to date, Ramsey in particular. He is a *players'* manager, and totally so. For all his officer-class affectations, he is at home with his troops and expects only two things from them: their commitment and their compliance. So long as these are forthcoming, he plays straight with them and shields them from the cruellest barbs of outsiders. The players, knowing how the press can turn on them, are thankful for that. And although none, not even the most established, can claim to be Ramsey's intimate, or to feel sure enough of his approval to relax completely in his company, even the bolshiest respects him.

It helps that Ramsey's already scaled most of the peaks he is asking them to climb. He's played thirty-two times for England between 1948 and 1953, making the right-back position his own. He's run out for his country with some of its legends – Tom Finney, Stanley Matthews, Wilf Mannion, Stanley Mortensen, Jackie Milburn, Nat Lofthouse, Billy Wright – and he's seen those legends cut down. There have been two defeats of symbolic horror since the Second World War: in the World Cup of 1950 in Brazil, when England were horribly embarrassed, beaten by the odd goal against the nonentities of the United States; and in 1953 when Hungary defeated them at Wembley by six goals to three. Ramsey played in both, and didn't like it.

The manager is a patriot of the contemporary kind. He believes in and admires characteristics now widely held to be innate in the true Englishman: phlegmatism, durability, loyalty, guts. Early on in his job, he'd looked ahead to 1966 and given the press his views on rival nations' teams. Some, he conceded, might have superior skills and a capacity for quicker thought. But that didn't mean their edge wouldn't be blunted by English conditions, the English atmosphere, the English spirit. He believes this. Yet at the same time he doesn't empathize with the Dunkirk corner of the English mythology which makes a virtue of muddling through. In a rare moment of incaution, Ramsey also said something which was reported as an assertion that England would win in 1966. To his dismay, he is now routinely forced to repeat this opinion, for it is not a position from which he can retreat without making things worse. Ramsey has apologized to the players for sparking off the pressure that's been put on them as a consequence. It was the last thing he wanted to happen. Ramsey believes in planning, not pontification.

He's a plotter, and cagey with it. It all increases the mystery. Some things about him don't add up. He prides himself on his appearance: suit and tie, collar and cuffs straight out of a Square Deal Surf commercial. But he also likes westerns, and he's always dragging the players off to see one. Then there's the beginning of a whisper that he pretended to be two years younger than his true age when he was a player. And why does he talk like a toff? He isn't born to it: although Ramsey's earliest years were spent in the half-rural Dagenham yet to be colonized by Londoners seeking council houses and production-line work for Henry Ford, his origins were plain. His dad was a small-time straw and hay dealer, his home a humble cottage. Local word has it that the

Ramseys are descended from gypsies, and Alf does have a vaguely Central European look about him which, combined with the jet hair of his youth, for a time earned him the nickname 'Darkie'.

But Ramsey will not be drawn on his suspected flight from his roots. Whether through shame, snobbery or just a deep reserve, mention of Dagenham seems to some to make him tense. His football past, though, speaks lucidly for itself. He was signed by Southampton of the Second Division while in the army and turned professional after the war. Converted from an inside-forward into a right full-back he thrived, winning his first England cap. When injury threatened his first-team place, he transferred to Tottenham Hotspur. Spurs were also in Division Two, but unlike Southampton they were ready to rise, and to heights no one had predicted. In 1950 they were promoted, and they won the First Division championship the following year.

It was an amazing feat, and Ramsey was crucial to it. At Spurs they called him the 'General', partly because of his passion for talking strategy off the pitch, partly because of the way he directed operations on it. Under manager Arthur Rowe, Spurs perfected a team technique called 'push and run', all short passes, neat triangles and timed runs into space. It was pretty to watch, painful to oppose and perfectly suited to Alf Ramsey's strengths. He was neither quick nor lithe, but he was studious, immaculate and calm. Ramsey loved playing under Rowe, loved talking football with him. He stayed at Spurs until he retired in 1955.

Management beckoned, irresistibly. Ipswich Town

were in the southern section of Division Three, a rural club with no history of achievement, little money and no mystique. But two years after Ramsey arrived they were promoted. Four years after that, they won the Second Division championship and the following year (season 1961–2) they won the first. These consecutive triumphs echoed those of the Tottenham side for which Ramsey had played, and the similarity was underlined by Ipswich's innovative approach. Ramsey's achievement was to make prosaic players perform wonders in unconventional roles. He had forward players lying deeper, and full-backs joining the attack. Opponents couldn't cope.

Ramsey evolved rapidly at Ipswich. Some, including those England players who found his speaking style amusing, thought the club's top brass were responsible for him falling for nob argot. Ipswich chairman John Cobbold was an eccentric Old Etonian, a man whose definition of a crisis – for press consumption at least – was finding the white wine served in the boardroom to be inadequately chilled. Perhaps it was Cobbold who'd introduced Alf to the pleasures of the occasional gin and tonic. Whatever, the future England manager had required little instruction in the art of keeping his feelings to himself. The day his team won the Second Division he declined to join the post-match party. But later that evening he sat in the empty grandstand alone except for his chairman. Handing Cobbold his jacket, he descended to the pitch and did a lap of honour on his own.

The summer that Ipswich were English champions,

the England team were knocked out of the World Cup by the eventual winners, Brazil. No shame in that, but it had been an uneven campaign. Walter Winterbottom had been manager since 1946 (Ramsey played all his internationals under him) and it was time to move on. His assistant Jimmy Adamson declined to step up, so the FA approached Ramsey. He named his terms, secured them, and accompanied the England team for the first time for an away match against France in February 1963. England lost five–two.

For the forty-five months which have elapsed since then, Alf Ramsey has been searching for the right players to win the cup in 1966. Some were already there, but finding all of them hasn't been easy. In his first season, Ramsey selected with circumspection. The veterans of Chile needed reinvigoration, but only two decisive changes were made. Johnny Haynes, Winterbottom's captain, was discarded. The team for Chile had been built around him, a quick, stylish inside-forward from Fulham. Haynes was the high-roller of English football, earning a hundred pounds a week. After the World Cup, he was injured in a car crash and missed the defeat by France. He recovered. But Ramsey never picked him.

The other important change came in goal. Ron Springett, a brave, bubbly Londoner who played for Sheffield Wednesday, was replaced by Gordon Banks of Leicester City after the defeat by France. Banks has been first choice ever since. He is twenty-eight, reliable, athletic, a pretty persistent talker to the defenders who play before him, and an absolute perfectionist. Banks comes from Sheffield, the son of a steelworker turned small-time bookmaker. He left school at fifteen, got a job bagging and delivering coal and then an apprenticeship as a bricklayer. He was spotted in the amateur leagues by Chesterfield, who signed him as a semi-professional then lost him to national service. Banks was stationed in Germany, where he met his wife. When he came back, he turned fully professional and earned the maximum wage of seventeen pounds a week. Banks' sloping eyebrows fill his features with the pathos of a clown. The others call him 'Fernandel' after the French film comedian. He is one of the four regular members of Ramsey's England teams who most pundits rate as world class, players who would win a place in just about any football team. The other three are Bobby Charlton, Jimmy Greaves and Bobby Moore.

Charlton is the most romantic figure. He has a sad face, thinning hair and a gentle air which inspires sympathy. He is a lovely footballer, an easy, graceful runner with the ball who can unleash clean, hard shots at goal with either foot while running at speed. He's from Ashington, a pit village in Northumberland, and football is in his blood. His mother Cissie has four brothers who all played for league teams, and Jackie Milburn, Newcastle United's intrepid centre-forward for many seasons, is her cousin. When Charlton was a teenager and his dad was down a mine, she gave him sprinting practice in the park and humoured the procession of men from professional clubs who came to her door offering fat wads if only her boy Bobby would sign up with them. The Charlton family is well endowed with football talent. Bobby's elder brother Jack is also in the squad. He plays centre-half for hard old Leeds United, and is a very different kettle of fish. Jack is a stroppy one: he'll have an argument with his own shadow.

But Bobby plays for the glamorous Manchester United. The association helps ensure that it isn't just his skills that make him appear blessed. One of the youngest of the Busby Babes, he survived the Munich air crash. When goalkeeper Harry Gregg found him in a puddle on the runway he thought he must be dead. But Charlton's injuries were slight. He lived, and the joy of his play, his modesty, his good grace under pressure, is all the more affecting because of his scrape with the reaper. He's twenty-eight now and Ramsey has improved him. This season, he's moved Charlton from outside-left to a more pivotal, creative position in the middle of the field. Charlton's critics complain that he has too many off days and is tactically naive. But the same sense of freedom reminds others of how glad they are that both they and Bobby Charlton are alive.

Jimmy Greaves has more of a swagger. He's a striker, a poacher, a flashing blade. He began in top football for Chelsea at just seventeen and became a scoring sensation. He is quick, clever, cocksure and prolific. His goals might be the finale of a fizzing dribble, or the apparently effortless consequence of his subtle anticipation, sharp control and swift dashes into vacant space. He's been an England star since scoring on his début in May 1959 and prior to Ramsey's appointment he'd scored twenty-two goals in twenty-six games. Like Ramsey, Greaves was born in Dagenham, later moving to nearby Hainault. But unlike the England manager he makes no attempt to erase the marks of his background. Greaves wears his raven hair slicked back, cracks disrespectful jokes and laughs like a Dagenham drain.

But for all his chat and dazzle, Greaves hasn't always been a winner. When the pressures have been greatest or the circumstances trying, he has been known to fail. In 1961 he became one of a select few British players to be signed by an opulent Italian club, Milan. He stayed for a few months and was miserable. Greaves couldn't speak the language or handle the ever-ravenous press. His manager criticized his attitude, his wife had her bottom pinched. So he returned to England, joining Spurs for a penny short of a hundred thousand pounds. In Chile too he had disappointed, scoring just once in four unexceptional games. Ramsey knows his gifts and admires them, but he also knows that Greaves, now twenty-six, can be mercurial and that his muse can betray him. He also knows that 'Greavsie' likes a drink. But he's kept on picking him: twenty-three times out of thirty-four matches up to the point the World Cup squad was named, and it would have been more but for injury and illness. Greaves has missed much of the 1965–6 season with jaundice. But he's scored thirteen goals for Ramsey. He's still a phenomenon. He is one of those at Lilleshall who knows he will not be left out.

Then there's Bobby Moore. He's a great mate of Greaves but a calmer man, commandingly so. Compounding coincidence, he too was born on the capital's eastern fringe, in Barking, which Dagenham adjoins. Moore comes from a respectable working-class south

Essex family. On Friday nights, his proud parents would help prepare him for the following day's schoolboy game, making sure he looked his best. His dad would polish his boots. His mum would iron his laces. As a young professional with West Ham United, Moore soon impressed as an unusual amalgam of application, intelligence and charisma. Although outstanding as a youth, Moore was considered slow, while his adolescent chubbiness earned him the insult 'tubby'. And when he first joined West Ham he lacked confidence. Yet he broke into the first team in 1958 while still in his teens. He remained short of great pace but the excess flesh had fallen away to reveal an immaculate, upright physique. Moore prospered by anticipation as well as by effort, and his tackles were distinguished more by their finesse than their ferocity.

He hasn't really changed. When he runs, his steps are short and he carries his shoulders up and his arms low. He holds his head high, pulls his shirt cuffs down over his wrists and passes the ball with studied precision, often over long distances. There is a mannered quality about his play, yet he oozes elegance. Ramsey made him England captain in May 1964 at the age of twenty-two, the youngest ever. He is tall, blond and unhurried. When the ball comes to Bobby Moore, no one looks away.

Things haven't always been easy between him and Ramsey, though. Moore's second match as captain was away to Portugal. The night before flying out, the England party gathered at the Hendon Hall hotel in the suburbs of north London. Moore, Greaves, Banks, Bobby Charlton, George Eastham, full-back Ray Wilson and one of Moore's West Ham colleagues, Johnny Byrne, went down town for a drink. The domestic season had just ended, and West Ham had won the FA Cup. A few bevvies wouldn't hurt. They headed for a bar called the Beachcomber which sold drinks called things like the Zombie and kept baby alligators in a tank. Wilson, a bit of a joker, lobbed them a few ice-cubes. But when the players returned to their rooms, each found his passport laid meaningfully on his bed. And when the squad stepped on to the training ground in Lisbon, Ramsey tore a strip off them. Fortunately, England went on to win four–three. Then, a fortnight later, the team went to New York to play the USA prior to a four-cornered tournament in Brazil dubbed the Little World Cup. Neither Moore nor Greaves was due to play, so they went out to see Ella Fitzgerald in concert. At breakfast, the manager cut them dead.

But these backstage hitches didn't seem to make any difference to Ramsey's opinion of the pair as players. They remained integral to a team which was looking a class act, having lost only once in its previous twelve matches on the eve of the Little World Cup. Then England met Brazil in Rio. Greaves scored, but it was England's only strike. The world champions got five. The next game was against Portugal again, whom they'd beaten in the friendly just seventeen days before. This time they only drew. Finally, they met Argentina, a steely, sophisticated outfit with a preference for defence who stole the only goal. England left the field feeling that they'd always been in the driving seat yet somehow lost the race. But whichever way the results of the Little World Cup were read, their lesson was the same: England had met the best and struggled.

The following season Ramsey tried some different permutations: four new centre-forwards, assorted wingers, numerous combinations in midfield. He picked a wiry little redhead from Blackpool, Alan Ball. Intermittently he persisted with Byrne, Southampton's Terry Paine, the experienced Ron Flowers of Wolverhampton Wanderers (normally his first reserve centre-half), Eastham of Stoke City, and from Liverpool Gordon Milne, Peter Thompson and Roger Hunt, the latter deputizing for Greaves. He revived the prospects of John Connelly, a goalscoring winger who'd gone to Chile but hadn't played and had since moved from Burnley to Manchester United. He gave a chance to Chelsea's Terry Venables, yet another player from Dagenham, but it was not one of the great romances. Venables's dad knew Ramsey's former next-door neighbour, a chap called Sid. At training, when Venables passed on Sid's regards Ramsey turned on his heel and stalked away. Greaves remained first-choice striker, but his ideal partner had not been settled on, and Bobby Charlton was still being used on the wing. One year before the World Cup, Ramsey didn't have his offensive forces sorted out at all.

His vision of a perfect defence, though, formed suddenly against Scotland, who visited Wembley in April 1965 to take part in the annual setpiece grudge match. It was the first international of that spring. Banks played as usual, as did Moore. The full-backs were George Cohen on the right and Ray Wilson on the left. Neither has looked like losing his primacy since. Cohen is a Londoner who plays for Fulham. He got his first chance as an international in 1964 after the incumbent, Blackpool's Jimmy Armfield, was seriously injured just before the Little World Cup. Armfield was the England captain then, and might still be but for their cruel misfortune which also brought about his replacement by Moore as skipper. A fine, experienced player with a great knowledge of the game, he's at Lilleshall and should be one of the lucky twenty-two, but the easygoing Cohen, a terse tackler with a surprising turn of speed, looks set for the number-two shirt. Wilson of Everton, recent winners of a dramatic FA Cup Final, has been an England man since 1960 and became so the hard way. Born in a pit village near Mansfield, his mother christened him Ramon (pronounced 'Ramm-on') after the Mexican Hollywood film star Ramon Navarro. As a child his parents split up and his mother, who brought him up alone, died when he was fifteen. Wilson worked fixing rolling stock in the local railyard until Huddersfield Town took him on. His progress was slow, and made slower by national service. But by 1959 he was a first-team regular, getting a bus to near the ground every home Saturday, then chatting to the fans as he walked the rest of the way. He is a gristly competitor and better versed in football's finer arts than full-backs are usually assumed to be.

Ramsey also blooded some new men, and two of them have stuck around. One was Jack Charlton. 'Big Jack' is six feet one, a tough tackler and a defender whose attitude to the ball when it is in his penalty area is to clear it first and ask questions later, most of them directed at any team mate within earshot whom Charlton believes responsible for the ball being near him in the first place. He is deep into his career now, past thirty, and he's never looked much like an athlete: his backside seems too big and his neck seems too long. He gets likened unkindly to a giraffe, though never by anyone he might turn round and get hold of. But appearances deceive. Charlton is indestructible, and he can leap higher than most from a standing position. He is strong where Moore is weakest. Moore is a poor header and sometimes gets punished for fancy foot-work. Ramsey thinks Charlton doesn't really trust Moore, and the feeling completes his liking for the combination.

The other successful débutant was Manchester United's Nobby Stiles. He came to international football with a bit of a reputation, and it hasn't gone away. If his club team is seen as English football's dashing cavaliers, Stiles is the court executioner. A former altar boy, he has grown up into five feet and six inches of indefatigable hostility deployed in the rougher pastures of midfield. His family background is Irish, Labour-voting and Catholic, his dad is an Oldham undertaker. In his first few seasons with United, Stiles interred some florid reputations with an irreducible, persistent aggression which displeased referees. Off the pitch his receding hair and heavy-framed spectacles give him the look of a permanently junior bank clerk. But in the dressing room before kick-off he inserts contact lenses and removes his false front teeth. And on the pitch, transformed, he scuffles, scrambles and spoils to the delight of his team mates and the displeasure of aesthetes. The latter's objections count for nothing in Ramsey's eyes. Stiles has stayed.

The match against Scotland was drawn, but it was the best result England had had against them under Ramsey. At that point he'd suffered just four defeats in twenty-one matches, but Scotland had inflicted half of these reverses. Ramsey was not amused, not least because of the particular pleasure the Scots and their fans took in such results. So when England went to Glasgow the following April and won four–three he derived a special satisfaction from the triumph. Results that season had been variable. England had lost at home to Austria and when they defeated West Germany at Wembley by a dull one–nil – Stiles was the unlikely scorer – some of their own fans had booed them from the field. But there'd been a sharp win over Spain in Madrid, the most impressive deployment yet of the novel 4–3–3 formation, and the Glasgow scoreline had flattered the vanquished. It also recommended others in an England line-up which, compared with many in the previous season, was unusual both in composition and in approach.

The defence was the regular one, except that Wilson was rested to give Keith Newton of Blackburn Rovers a go. But Ball – 'Little Bally' – had functioned again as a sort of flank midfielder with Bobby Charlton in the centre wearing 9 for the first time. Connelly, enjoying a flush of good form, had also played. Greaves was ill, but Hunt had scored twice in his absence. He was partnered in attack by West Ham's Geoff Hurst, who also scored, playing only his second England game. Bobby Charlton got the other goal. All very satisfactory, except for one moment involving Connelly to which Ramsey drew everyone's attention when he replayed a film of the game to them later.

Hampden Park, Glasgow, has a broad running track around the pitch. The ball went out for a throw-in to Scotland and Connelly, having fetched it by the perimeter fence, generously knocked it to an opponent waiting at the touch line. The opponent thanked him for his kindness by immediately throwing it to the full-back Connelly should have been marking. A goal almost resulted, and Connelly, realizing his error, had been fretting ever since. Alf never forgot. Now nemesis approached. 'Look at this,' said Ramsey, pointing at the projection screen as the incident unfolded. 'Look what that fucking pillock did.' It wasn't often that Ramsey swore, but the Scots liberated his suppressed vernacular like few other opponents could. The shock effect of this lapse into blueness was underlined by the bizarreness of his accent. And everybody got the message: Alf Ramsey's England gives *nothing* away, not one fucking thing.

At Lilleshall, the heartache moment approaches. Ramsey takes his rejects aside one by one, and breaks the bad news to them gently but plainly in his stiff Queen's English. Milne is out, Thompson is out, Newton is out, Bobby Tambling of Chelsea is out and so is Johnny Byrne. Byrne is such a habitually chirpy chatterbox that everyone calls him 'Budgie'. Now poor

Budgie shuts right up, as if someone has tossed a towel over his cage. It's hard on him, but football's like that. There is no come-back, no redress, nothing to do except go home and be brave and perhaps, in darker moments, hope that one of the other lads breaks a leg.

Two

Sunday, 10 July 1966

THE REST of the world has arrived. There's never been anything like it. Brazilians have descended on Merseyside and they're doing the samba in the streets. Germans have been sighted in Sheffield, and Spanish is being spoken in the pubs of Birmingham. In Sunderland, Italians are settling in to the International Club, specially founded to make foreign guests feel wanted. In nearby Middlesbrough, the local World Cup liaison committee is welcoming a handful of impeccably mannered North Koreans. It's a diplomatic task: the British government has refused to recognize their nascent nation's existence, their flag has been expunged from a set of commemorative postage stamps, and the North Atlantic Treaty Organization has objected to their flag being flown. Having been so comprehensively insulted they are shortly to get stuffed at football. Meanwhile, in the capital, Mexicans in huge sombreros are shaking their maracas. Tourism is one thing. This is something else.

The one million all-purpose, sixty-four-page World Cup programmes have been printed, each containing the names of every member of each of the sixteen com-

peting squads. There have been a few hitches. The programme was to include a message of welcome from the
FA chairman Joe Mears, who wrote it before heading
off on the England tour of Scandinavia, but he died on
1 July after his piece had gone to press. Last-minute
adjustments were swiftly made. The final list of players
was made available to the printers – McCorquodale
and Company – only late on 4 July, and tomorrow
evening England will play Uruguay at Wembley in the
opening game.

For the football authorities the big kick-off will
mark the culmination of four years of pondering, planning and advance cost-management. Making a World
Cup work is no automatic process. The Chileans built
two splendid new stadiums in honour of the occasion,
but many of the matches were played in run-down
grounds before embarrassingly tiny crowds. The cost in
terms of both finance and credibility has not been lost
on the FA hierarchy, a proud and conservative group of
men. Their ambitions for their own World Cup are
straightforward: they will make it impressive and they
will make it pay.

Succeeding really matters. English football has
developed symptoms of long-term decline. League
crowds have shrunk dramatically since the war, from
around a hundred million to nearer thirty million a
season now. The boom years have given ordinary people
other things to do with their Saturday afternoons: they
have gardens to tend, Austin A40s to drive and patios
to lay. Football's near-monopoly on the non-drinking
(though often post-drinking) leisure hours of the

working-class English male is eroding, and a glorious home World Cup will help reassert the status of the national game. But even beginning to achieve this has meant taking some shrewd financial decisions and facing some unfortunate facts about the more distinctive characteristics of the English football culture.

The earliest crucial decisions concerned the selection of venues. These, it was quickly grasped, would have to be large, widely spread and equipped with facilities likely to find favour with an influx of aliens whose quantity and cosmopolitanism the island nation will not have previously experienced. Although the full list of qualifiers would not become known until late in 1965, the general expectations of the majority of foreign visitors could be guessed at with some confidence. Western Europe would supply the bulk, and their spectating experiences would be quite different from those of most of the English fans. Over there, beyond the Channel, fans expect to sit and watch a game. But in England the great all-male majority stand and sway on staggered Victorian terraces that are often as open to the elements as the toilets their patrons rush to at half-time, where they leak hurriedly against communal walls and watch the steam rise pungently towards bleak winter skies. All this must be improved on.

After a fashion, the necessary eight grounds were picked. None has a capacity of less than 50,000, even though substantial numbers of additional seats have temporarily invaded the standing paddocks and beloved terracing. None of the pitches measures less than 115 yards long and 75 yards wide, as required by the Fédération Internationale de Football Association, the world game's ruling body. This has ruled out Arsenal's ground in Highbury, north London, which is thirteen and a half feet short. There are no Arsenal players in Alf Ramsey's squad either, so the rejection of the Gunners' handsome citadel ensures that one of English football's most august centres of soccer power will play no part in the drama to come other than to make its undersized pitch available for the England squad to train on.

Everton's Goodison Park in north Liverpool was also a few yards lacking, in both directions. But in this case there was enough spare space round the edge to lay some extra turf. And in another respect, Goodison stood head and shoulders above the other club grounds: it has one hundred and twenty seats in its press box, making it easily the biggest. Most have no more than forty, and accommodating the media masses at stadiums built in the previous century presented a major challenge. At least four hundred pressmen are now expected at every game, and a thousand for the final. Each one has had to be provided with two feet and three inches of working space compared with the usual foot-and-a-half. And apart from an extra nine inches, they also require complex communications technology: additional telephone lines have been connected, telex facilities have been installed. The cost has run into thousands. Now the hacks have arrived, swarms of them. They are from all sixteen competing nations, but also from Luxembourg and Tunisia, from Mauritius and Sudan. From just about everywhere.

The opening phase of the competition has the sixteen

teams divided into four self-contained mini-leagues or groups, and each programme of group fixtures will be played in a different part of the country. All the Group One matches will be at Wembley except for one, to be held at the White City athletics stadium on the capital's western outskirts, venue of the 1948 Olympic Games. England and Uruguay are in Group One, along with Mexico and France. Uruguay have an auspicious World Cup record. They hosted and won the inaugural World Cup in 1930, won it again in 1950 and are still a formidable force from what, to English eyes, has lately become the heart of football darkness, South America.

Goodison Park is one of the two venues for Group Three and the other is Old Trafford, home of Manchester United. The north-west group is the most eye catching. It contains the champions Brazil, complete with their sumptuous superstar Pelé, the 'Black Pearl', the greatest player in the world. They are joined by Portugal, whose scintillating striker Eusebio of the great club side Benfica is also universally revered, and by Hungary, the communist bloc's only acknowledged soccer poets. Bulgaria, the latter's neighbours from behind the Iron Curtain, look like making up the numbers.

Group Two should be lively too. This is described, semi-anomalously, as the midlands group. Villa Park, Birmingham, Aston Villa's ground, is one of its two venues, but the other is Sheffield Wednesday's Hillsborough, and citizens of South Yorkshire do not normally recognize themselves as midlanders. Ah well, they've got some high-grade football to look forward to. There's

Spain, boasting Luis Suarez, for whom Internazionale of Milan paid a world-record £200,000. There's West Germany, captained by national hero Uwe Seeler and dubbed in one pre-tournament souvenir book as the World Cup's 'dark horses'. And there's Argentina, who are 'South American' like Uruguay but better and, worryingly, possibly better than England too. Switzerland are the lambs awaiting slaughter.

Only in the north-east, where Group Four will take place, is there a shortage of soccer aristocrats. Italy alone boast a handsome pedigree, and their club football has acquired the habit of extreme defensiveness. The USSR (it is muttered darkly) are basically the footballing equivalent of Alexei Kosygin's Cold War army, and expected to be every bit as drab and ruthless. Chile are from South America but they don't even have a lurid reputation as swarthy assassins with which to excite the xenophobic. And what about North Korea, the one representative of Asia? Could be painful, couldn't it?

This allocation of teams to groups and the order and location of the fixtures within them emerged from the World Cup Draw ceremony, held in the Palace Suite of the newly completed Royal Garden Hotel in west London's smart Kensington High Street on 6 January. Two multinational rows of FIFA officials wearing sober suits and ties and fronted by FIFA's English president Sir Stanley Rous sat in panel formation behind a row of silver trophies numbered 1 to 4. Before them, eight hundred eager onlookers gathered, half of them football officials and players, half of them journalists. In the gallery, radio broadcasters chattered in a plethora of foreign tongues. Television cameras panned and pored. Football was confirming its tenancy in the developing global village.

As well as discharging a necessary duty, the draw ceremony was a giant promotional exercise with the aim of convincing the many millions monitoring the event at home and around the globe that the coming competition was sure to enthrall. Guaranteeing this was, of course, impossible. But certain steps had already been taken towards stirring the maximum anticipation. The first phase of the competition is designed to cut the field by half, with the top two sides of the four groups going through to four quarter-final play-offs. So the winners of Group One will play the runners-up of Group Two, and the runners-up of Group One will play the winners of Group Two. The same formulation will apply to the winners and runners-ups of Groups Three and Four. But the group line-ups were also engineered to keep certain teams and their substantial bands of ticket-buying, hotel-residing, hotdog-eating, souvenir-hunting supporters from playing each other too soon in the competition and risking half of them going home early along with their glamorous teams.

To this end, a seeding system was devised. All England's games were certain sell-outs, so in the service of both public interest and profit it was preordained that all their three group games will be played at Wembley, whose capacity of over 90,000 makes it easily the biggest ground. Brazil, the cup holders, were likewise seeded into Group Three to ensure that they cannot meet England until the semi-finals at the earliest. The rest of the draw was arranged so that remaining teams coming from the same continent were evenly spread among the groups in the hope of producing matches of maximum novelty and so that potential titanic clashes of giants (especially neighbouring ones) will be delayed until the stakes are higher. Thus the other three South American nations – Uruguay, Argentina and Chile – were seeded away from each other and from Brazil, as were the latin Europeans, Italy, Portugal and Spain.

This elaborate mechanism seems to have given the desired good last push to the sales and promotion efforts of the World Cup Organization, a body set up by the FA in 1963 for precisely those tasks and led by Chief Administrative Officer Mr Ken Willson. The Organization's small staff is accommodated away from the FA's Lancaster Gate HQ in a block of eight offices at the side of the White City stadium. Here, the uptake of different grades and combinations of the two million tickets available for the thirty-two World Cup matches is tracked on special blackboards with white chalk. Ten weeks after the draw, receipts topped the million-pound mark, a fortnight ahead of schedule.

This triumph is due to a sales operation based on a cunning market fix. The problem at the outset was to attract the biggest possible audiences for future football matches whose occurrence was assured but whose contestants and locations were almost all unknowable. The trick has been to make access to the matches most likely to be attractive dependent on also buying tickets for those less likely to appeal. For example, any World Cup final, whoever is playing, is a certain advance sell-out, so tickets for it have been sold in the first place only as part of a season ticket for no less than nine other matches as well, including one semi-final, one quarter-final, the third-and-fourth place play-off and six group matches of the buyer's choice, all to be viewed from an equivalent position in whichever venue the matches take place in. The most deluxe World Cup ticket of all secures the purchaser a seat in the main stand of any ground, at a cost of twenty-five pounds and ten shillings. A ten-match season for the cheapest part of a ground is a more affordable three pounds, seventeen shillings and sixpence. Maybe most of the matches won't hold great interest for such ticket-buyers. But the theory is that, since they've already paid, they'll feel that they might just as well go.

Other season tickets cover seven, four or three games, the first two types sold on the hook of a quarter-final, the last securing entrance to group matches only. (Purchasers of any of these 'seasons' were also entitled to enter a ballot for surplus places available for the final. These resulted from the decision to sell tickets for the final to the general public only as part of a season ticket encompassing matches at smaller grounds as well. It meant that the total number of season tickets covering the final could only be as great as the capacity of the smallest World Cup venue, rather than that of Wembley, which has by far the largest.) A proportion of all these configurations was first made available – eighteen months in advance – to potential visitors from overseas on the basis that they were the people whose need for

advance planning – time off, travel and hotel accommodation – was the greatest. More than forty thousand
took up the option, and were surely intrigued to notice
that English football was among the cheapest to watch
anywhere in the western world.

Television has also helped to build momentum, and
the medium is set to excel itself in terms of scale
and style of coverage. There will be crews from all over
the globe, and the BBC and its commercial rival ITV
have joined together to provide the necessary equipment
for all the visiting broadcasting companies. But they
will also compete for viewers, and the BBC has given
over an unprecedented proportion of its schedule to live
World Cup games. As a result all manner of regular,
popular mid-evening programmes have been postponed
for the bulk of July. Many viewers are displeased, but
the choice had to be made: if only the BBC had a second
channel. But at each of the eight grounds camera sites
have been constructed and commentary positions
fashioned. Every match will be filmed and coverage
will be co-ordinated from Television Centre, Shepherd's
Bush. Bryan Cowgill, Head of the BBC TV Sport, is
going to be a busy man.

The Corporation knows all about big outside-broad-
cast events and the appeal of televised sport. It's already
covered everything from the Coronation of Queen
Elizabeth II at Westminster Abbey in 1953, to the Olympic Games in Tokyo eleven years later. Rights to the
1966 World Cup were negotiated with FIFA shortly
after England was named as the venue back in 1960,
and were sold as part of a deal which also obliged

the BBC to televise the 1962 competition. The public appetite was duly whetted. When Peter Dimmock, the BBC's Head of Outside Broadcasts, announced details of the 1966 coverage, he and his colleagues knew perfectly well that they were dealing with a massive national event of international importance. The BBC's achievement, Dimmock predicted, would be to make the World Cup spectacle 'a valuable shop window for this country'.

The BBC has got the team to do it. Jimmy Hill, the former chairman of the Professional Footballers' Association whose leadership had been essential to the ending of the maximum wage, has proved himself an able television communicator. During the World Cup preview programme he will present an explanation of the offside law, largely with lady viewers in mind. The Wembley anchor-man will be the bright young David Coleman. Commentator Kenneth Wolstenholme is the acknowledged master of his craft, and he will be assisted by an impressive technical innovation which will enable viewers to look again at significant passages of play in slow motion only seconds after they've happened. It's called the 'action replay', and the machine that makes it possible arrived from the United States only three weeks ago.

The BBC's enthusiasm has been a blessing for the FA and FIFA. Apart from the press, television has been the only major vehicle through which they have been able to take their product to the public. Despite hopeful canvassing, no major private companies have come forward with endorsements or financial support. The

Royal Garden Hotel has been the one exception, offering its Palace Suite free of charge. The FA has been unable to afford an advertising campaign of any kind. Instead, it has published 100,000 posters and asked nicely if anyone would mind putting them up. From the domestic public sector, only British Rail has obliged. English football clubs have attached them to noticeboards. A few airlines, sensing potential custom, have done the same. Each poster is adorned with the official tournament insignia designed by Arthur Bew, a commercial artist who lost a leg in the Second World War. It comprises a representation of the trophy against the background of a football depicted as the globe, all superimposed on to a Union Jack. The use of the Union flag to denote an event to take place exclusively in England illustrates a distinctively English attitude towards the other parts of the British Isles with which it is constitutionally linked. The flag of England is the cross of St George. The Union Jack is an amalgamation of this and the flags of Scotland and Northern Ireland (though not of Wales, which is assumed in this context to be merely an adjunct of England). Quite apart from being inaccurate, depicting England and the rest of the United Kingdom as synonymous demonstrates a commonplace assumption of English superiority over its neighbours. But such considerations do not seem to have exercised the FA.

The same conflation is repeated in a second World Cup symbol, commissioned with a view to commercial exploitation. It's a sturdy cartoon lion. He wears football boots, shorts and a Union-Jack football shirt. This amiable figure has been created by Reginald Hoye, an artist with Walter Tuckwell and Associates, the company retained to negotiate licences for the use of World Cup insignia on souvenir goods. The connection was arranged by the World Cup Organization, whose leader Mr Willson had been dubbed 'World Cup Willie' by his staff. Someone remarked that Mr Willson had a similar physique to the friendly little lion. The nickname duly passed from administrator to cartoon.

World Cup Willie is now regularly seen in the popular newspapers, striking a variety of poses. He's even appeared in a kilt, weeping (presumably fraternally), the day after Scotland's last hope of appearing in the final series disappeared one December evening in Naples. Likenesses of Willie also adorn around a hundred items of World Cup merchandise ranging from braces to glove puppets, from horse-brasses to handkerchiefs. There is even a song about him. World Cup fever is definitely spreading, refreshing interest in the ancient national game. With its deep roots and stubborn habits, football is in many ways stuck in England's past. Yet despite its shrunken audience, it remains hugely popular and so an integral part of English – and British – life, still ingrained in urban communities of working people everywhere.

This has never been lost on Harold Wilson, a former grammar schoolboy and Meccano enthusiast from Milnsbridge, near Huddersfield, who in October 1964 was elected Prime Minister and formed Britain's first Labour government since Clement Attlee's straight after the war. Although Wilson's victory was narrow – his majority was just five seats – it was seen as reflecting a deep national desire for modernization and change after thirteen years of Conservative rule. Labour's manifesto was entitled *The New Britain*, and its campaign message focused on the youth, vision and popular appeal of its brilliant leader. Eager to be seen to share the passions of the people, Wilson created the new position of Minister with Special Responsibility for Sport and offered the job to the MP for Birmingham Small Heath, Denis Howell, a qualified football referee with a knack for generating publicity.

When he was summoned to Number 10 Downing Street, Howell knew nothing of Wilson's plans. Nervously, he waited outside his office while on the other side of the door the PM and his most senior colleagues tried to decide whether the economy was in such a dreadful state that they would have to devalue the pound. When finally called to his leader's desk and told of his historic appointment, Howell expressed appropriate gratitude and asked the new premier what policy he should pursue. Wilson responded by telling Howell that this was for him to decide: after all, he added, if he'd thought Howell didn't know what to do he would never have given him the job. Howell said thank-you again, though he wasn't quite sure what for. He then asked how much money he would be given to spend. Wilson told him he would have none at all, but consoled Howell with the thought that having no money to spend meant he had more time to think things over.

So Howell thought about that. Then he said to Wilson: 'Did you know we've got the World Cup in

'66?' Wilson had been promoted as a sports enthusiast, a man whose childhood happiness had been intimately connected with the fortunes of Yorkshire County Cricket Club and Huddersfield Town FC. Presumably, then, it took some effort to suppress a note of boyish enthusiasm when he asked the new minister for sport what the World Cup was. Howell explained: it was an international football tournament for the world's sixteen top soccer nations. The elite exponents of the greatest game would be jetting in. They would bring with them officials, journalists and fans, entourages running into thousands. Facilities would have to be provided, public interest serviced, protocols observed. It was important that Labour Britain should be seen to put on a good show. All right, all right, said the dynamic Harold Wilson. How much do you want? Howell hadn't the slightest idea. 'Half a million pounds,' he said, straight off the top of his head. 'Right, you can have half a million pounds,' replied Wilson, 'and not a penny more.'

Half a million pounds was a tidy sum. Sir John Lang, Howell's permanent secretary, a top civil servant who'd worked for Winston Churchill during the war, told him that Her Majesty's Treasury would never wear it – half a million pounds, for *football*? Governments did not normally concern themselves with such matters. Howell pointed out that since the Prime Minister was also First Lord of the Treasury, the Treasury would *have* to wear it. The really pressing question was: how should it be spent? This was a trickier question to answer than it appeared. At first it seemed that the money would not, after all, become available. But in February 1965 it was finally sanctioned, by which time most of the preparatory work for the World Cup had already been put in hand and paid for. The stadiums had been upgraded and the ticketing operation was in full swing. The government was only offering to subsidize improvements, not pay for them outright. The FA had already insisted that host clubs would have to increase the amount of seating available, and the cost of this had largely been met from their own pockets.

Howell set off on a tour of World Cup grounds to see what else could be done, accompanied by Sir Stanley Rous, Denis Follows, the FA secretary, Ron Greenwood, the civilized and studious manager of West Ham, and some chaps in bowler hats. His first request on being greeted by club chairmen was to be shown to the ladies' toilets. It was a running joke, but it had a serious purpose. Howell was aware that groups of foreign fans were likely to include substantially more women than any English football crowd. As a representative of the Crown it was his duty to ensure that no visiting *fräulein* or *señorita* would have to endure the special indignities of a stinking English privy.

Fortunately Howell's horizons were wider than ladies' lavatories. At Hillsborough, he agreed to help build an indoor fitness centre for Sheffield Wednesday players on condition that it was first used as a World Cup press room. At Everton he leaned on the local council to rehouse the residents of three council dwellings which impeded access to the ground and then demolish the buildings. Howell provided sums to the value of 90 per cent of the cost of ground improvements which would be permanent, four-fifths of it as a grant, the other fifth as a loan. The full half a million pounds was never spent, but more temporary seating was installed and facilities for formal receptions provided. As Howell and his companions roamed from ground to ground, the local press turned out in force. This was populist interventionist government at its most plain and effective, and it surely played its part in helping Harold Wilson get re-elected with a healthier majority on the last day of March this year.

But if Howell's success in making a link between the government and the World Cup gave a further impetus to public enthusiasm for both the contest and, indirectly, the Prime Minister, it was as nothing compared with the avalanche which followed unseen events at the Methodist Central Hall, Westminster, eleven days before Harold Wilson's re-election. After lengthy negotiations, FIFA had agreed to allow the World Cup itself – the Jules Rimet trophy, named after one of the two French co-founders of the tournament, the other being Henri Delaunay – to be exhibited on the Stanley Gibbons stand at the Stampex Exhibition.

What began as a philatelists' paradise suddenly turned into a football administrators' nightmare as the twelve-inch-high gold trophy was stolen while a religious service was being conducted in the same building. Ransom demands were telephoned to Joe Mears and the lid of the cup arrived at his home by post, sent in order to lend the enterprise an emphatic mark of authenticity.

Five days later the arrest was made of a man called Edward Bletchley, and two days after that a citizen named David Corbett claimed that his dog, an endearing mutt called Pickles, had found the trophy while sniffing under a hedge on Beulah Hill in Norwood, south London. Pickles, briefly, became the most photographed dog alive. Bletchley received a two-year stretch for his efforts, but before attending his hearing he made a statement to the press: 'Whatever my sentence is, I hope that England wins the World Cup.' And so say all of us.

Three

Monday, 11 July 1966

THE ENGLAND party gathers in Wembley Stadium's North dressing room at around six o'clock. Everyone who matters most is there: Ramsey, Shepherdson, Cocker, Bass, the eleven who are playing and the eleven who are not. To each other they demonstrate a collective relish for the challenge to come, and confidence in the outcome. This is no less genuine for the range of deep mixed feelings which burn beneath: concealed, keen disappointment for some of those not selected; churning tension for those who are.

Eleven shirts are arranged around the dressing-room walls in numerical order. The first six are as expected: 1 for Banks, 2 for Cohen, 3 for Wilson, 4 for Stiles, 5 for Jack Charlton, 6 for the captain, Moore. Not for the first time, there's been some disquiet about Moore. He's fallen out with his club over wages and only a temporary contract drawn up by Ron Greenwood has made him eligible to play in the World Cup matches. There's even been speculation about his place in Ramsey's team. For three of the first five matches of the calendar year it has been made over to Norman Hunter, Jack Charlton's abrasive partner in central defence at

Leeds. These included the opening game of the post-Lilleshall, pre-World Cup European tour in which England beat Finland three–nil. But, if some observers have suspected that Moore is on the brink of decommission, Hunter never has. He remains glad to be Moore's understudy – he loves working with Ramsey – and, as the captain changes into his kit, Hunter prepares to head off to his seat with the other reserves.

These include Geoff Hurst. He is the one surprising omission from the team, surprising not because he has become an automatic choice, but because of the number he was alloted after the squad of twenty-two was formally named. The players given numbers 1 to 11 are assumed to comprise Ramsey's first-choice team, and Hurst is number 10. Although he only made his début in February in the plodding one–nil victory over West Germany, he scored in the next game, which was the great rout of Scotland at Hampden, and he looks like the centre-forward Ramsey has been searching for. Hurst is the son of a professional footballer – Charlie Hurst was a wing-half in the lower divisions. His son is young – twenty-four – strong and athletic, sturdy on the ground and powerful in the air. Less obvious to the inexpert is his command of techniques which are increasingly important for players of his type in the modern game. Hurst excels at receiving the ball with his back to the opponents' goal. It may come rushing towards him through the air, at speed and at the most inconvenient height, but Hurst will shape to intercept it, accept it on his thigh or chest, deaden its momentum, and play it to a team mate without once flinching from the attentions of the opposing centre-half, who's pressing his hands down on his shoulders or sticking his knee into his back.

But in Scandinavia and Poland, Ramsey tried every combination of his three central front men, and Hurst fared the worst. Roger Hunt, by contrast, did well and by the time the tour was over he was averaging a goal a game for his twelve England matches. A haulier's son from Warrington, Hunt has his critics. Despite all he has achieved for both Liverpool and England, he is used to unflattering comparisons with Jimmy Greaves. He even accepts them, up to a point. Greaves *is* touched with genius, he can see that. Yet Hunt has enjoyed a successful spell deputizing for him during his illness and was mortified when given the number 21 shirt while the Tottenham man retained the number 8. But now Hunt is in for the Uruguay game, playing alongside Greaves rather than shadowing him.

Hunt loves playing for England, but he finds it quite exacting. In the old parlance, he sees himself as an inside-forward, a player who feeds off a centre-forward supplied by flying wingers. This is what happens at Liverpool, where he is part of a front four with Peter Thompson, Ian Callaghan (who, unlike the unfortunate Thompson, has joined Hunt in Ramsey's squad) and the Scottish centre-forward Ian St John. In many of his England games there has been only one winger, or even just a wide midfield player. This means that Hunt has to do more of what comes naturally to Hurst, and it can seem thankless. There's not much glory. But the other players appreciate his striving. So, it seems, does Ramsey, and he's the one who matters most.

Today, Hunt must be content with just one winger to help him. Number 11 is his room mate John Connelly. Like the other players in their later twenties, Connelly's career has coincided with all the big changes in the profession. He was born in St Helens, Lancashire, a stronghold of rugby league, and worked as a joiner in a coalmine. He signed with Burnley in late 1956 and his workaday job moved there with him: football was his passion, but still only part-time. He was still practising his joiner's trade on the side when he first played for England in 1959. Connelly's assets include the ability to function effectively on either side of the pitch. For England he is used to being free to rove, backing his own judgement of his prospects. In that way, Ramsey liberates him. And Connelly is overjoyed at being selected. He's been worrying about it. He hasn't forgotten 1962, when he travelled to Chile full of well-founded hope, but in the final analysis another was preferred. And for the last match of the spring tour he'd been replaced by Martin Peters, a quiet young midfielder from West Ham whom Ramsey hadn't ever picked before. But Hunt bet Connelly that he'd be back for the opening game. Now, at twenty-seven, he *is* back, and this is the greatest chance he's had as an international player.

At number 7 is Alan Ball. Twenty years old and five feet seven, he's the youngest and, apart from Stiles, the smallest in the team. Ball has been sweating up the 7 shirt for six of the last nine games (and the number 11 in a seventh) and he seems to have clinched his claim over the orthodox wingers who conventionally wear it. He is versatile: he can pass with crisp precision, he can outpace and centre, he can tackle, pester and harass. He seems unable to rest or give in and he is desperate to win, always has been. His hair is red and curly, his voice pipes. As a boy, growing up in Farnworth near Bolton, he'd been an unusual physical specimen. He was always small (still in short trousers at sixteen) and always compulsively demonstrating how he wasn't going to let that stop him. His father, a former player turned non-league manager, is his idol and a stern patriarch, always disapproving of every indulgence that might take a young man's fancy as memories of ration books faded. Fags were out, booze was out, girls were out. Ball is secretly engaged to the only girl he's ever dated. Otherwise, he has obeyed. But his deference to authority is not automatic, and he is capable of impassioned insubordination. As a teenager at Blackpool he dared to give some lip to the great Stanley Matthews: he just knew that Matthews was wrong. But to Ramsey he is biddable, loyal and inspired by a voluble love of country.

The eleventh player in the team is Bobby Charlton, wearing 9. No surprise there.

Substitutes are not allowed for World Cup matches, so the rest of the squad slips away to spectate: Hurst and Hunter; goalkeepers Springett and Peter Bonetti of Chelsea; full-backs Armfield and Liverpool's Gerry Byrne; Ron Flowers; George Eastham and Terry Paine the Southampton winger; Callaghan and Peters. They all wish they were playing. Watching will be hell. Ball talks, Hunt looks nervous, Jack Charlton sits in silence. Stiles goes through an elaborate preparation which would be funny to the others if this was a frivolous occasion. First he gets into his shorts and shirt, then he coats the inside of his boots with Vaseline. He soaks his feet in hot water, then pulls on his socks and boots. Off comes his shirt again, and he douses his chest and legs with olive oil, rubbing it in well before replacing the shirt, then knotting his tie-ups, then greasing his face and hands before going to a mirror. His eyes go in, his teeth come out and he carefully combs his hair. Others just warm up and pace about, their screw-in studs clack-clacking on the dressing-room floor. All they want to do is get out there and get on with it.

There's a knock on the door, summoning them into the tunnel leading out to the arena. Eighty-seven thousand spectators have been watching the opening ceremony as shadows lengthen: London schoolboys parading in the kit of the participating nations, military bandsmen marching. The big noise echoes down to the players, and the full magnitude of the occasion begins to take hold of their nerves. The England players line up, stretching and shuffling. The Uruguayans are there too, back at Wembley for the first time since May 1964 when England beat them two–one. Their recent form has been poor, and when one of their officials said at the draw ceremony that it was an honour to play England first, he was probably just being polite. Their manager Ondino Viera is frustrated that several of his regulars have not been released by the Argentinian clubs they play for, and his team is very young. But he's still got some classy performers. Ladislao Mazurkieviez is one of the best goalkeepers around, maybe as good as Banks. Captain Horacio Troche is a knowing defender. Pedro Rocha is their midfield *artiste*. These players have big hopes of progressing to the later stages, and a defeat in their first fixture will make the pressure on them heavy. They won't succumb without a struggle.

Outside there is a fanfare followed by a few queenly words from Elizabeth II: 'I welcome all our visitors and feel sure that we shall be seeing some fine football. It now gives me great pleasure to declare open the eighth world football championships.' On the stadium roof, the sixteen national flags – including North Korea's, from which the Foreign Office has agreed to avert its gaze – unfurl in unison, a triumph of manual co-ordination.

Now the players emerge from the tunnel in twin single files led by the match officials. All three are from eastern Europe. Istvan Zsolt of Hungary is the referee. His linesmen are Dimiter Roumentchev of Bulgaria, and Tofik Bakhramov from Azerbaijan, the Turkish-speaking part of the USSR. Behind them walk Ramsey and Viera. Then Moore and Troche. Jack Charlton brings up the rear of the England line. He *always* brings up the rear. Big Jack is particular that way. The captains are carrying footballs. These footballs have been manufactured by Slazengers Ltd. of Croydon, Surrey, whose product was chosen blind by members of the FIFA Bureau in the presence of the press in preference to the footballs of eight other British and European manufacturers. The players could not care less. They wish only to kick the things and take the edge of their tension away.

But first it's time to meet the monarch. Moore presents her with a bunch of flowers and then introduces the other players, leading the way along a broad red carpet: Cohen, Banks, Ball and so on down to the manager at the end. The Queen wears white gloves and a green and white straw hat and carries a handbag. Ramsey wears a suit, collar and tie. It's the first time he has ever appeared at an England match in anything other than a team tracksuit. The Queen moves across to the Uruguayans, the Duke of Edinburgh, Denis Howell, Sir Stanley Rous and the Earl of Harewood, the FA president, in tow. As she shakes hands with Troche, the other Uruguay players hop from Adidas to Adidas, Puma to Puma. The crowd looks on at the opposition men with their black hair and olive skins. Even the look of their kit promises a different way of doing things. It follows unfamiliar design rules. England's shirts are snow white, long-sleeved, crew-necked and decorated with a crest on the left breast which, as aficionados know, is graced with three prowling lions. Their shorts are black, their stockings white. All very simple, very clean, very pure. But the Uruguayans wear pale-blue shirts with v-necks and short sleeves, each finished with a white line of trim. Their shorts and socks are black. It's an odd combination, there's nothing like it here. Mazurkieviez wears pale grey. They are strangers from a small, hot country which English fans know little about except that the football is slow and cagey and worth getting resentful about.

The national anthems are trumpeted and the bandsmen wheel slowly away. As the other players break rank and begin kicking in, there's a centre-spot toss-up between Moore and Troche which Troche wins. The players change ends and the England supporters start raising the Wembley Stadium roof. They have a special clapping rhythm picked up from the Brazilian fans in Chile: one-two, one-two-three, one-two-three-four, ONE-TWO, and to the last one-two they add a simultaneous shout of 'ENG-LAND!'

It's a very southern crowd. This is a midweek evening and there's not much time for folk outside Greater London to get to Wembley after work in time for kick-off. (Just now, almost everyone's in work.) Automobile Association spotter planes have seen a huge build-up of traffic since about 5.45, and there's been a two-mile hold-up at the Greenford roundabout. They've piled down Olympic Way towards the famous twin towers wearing ribbon rosettes and boaters and top hats painted in the colours of the Union Jack. A few rotate enormous wooden rattles that sound like volleys of friendly machine-gun fire. Like Alf Ramsey, very many of them are wearing collars and ties. This is a 'great occasion, a big summer's evening out. There are policemen, but not many. Disorder is not expected. In South America, people die at football matches, players get attacked by fans, referees get shot. English people aren't like that.

The ball is on the centre spot. Next to it stand Bobby

Charlton and Jimmy Greaves. The referee's whistle blows. Charlton kicks off. England go on the attack. Wilson combines with Bobby Charlton down the left and Connelly, dashing goalwards, homes in on Charlton's centre as the crowd howls him on, gasping for the gratification of an early goal. But the Uruguayan defenders are back in numbers. Two of them close in. Connelly is crowded out. The Uruguayans, tense and circumspect, turn the ball away for a corner.

Connelly hustles down to the flag to take the kick, and as he does so Jack Charlton advances. Great height is not a feature of the England forwards – Hunt is the tallest at five foot nine – so Big Jack supplements them at set pieces. The corner comes over and is cleared for another. This is propelled back into play, and the ball breaks for Greaves out on the right who slips past two defenders and crosses the ball towards Hunt. But Hunt is a lone white figure in a pale-blue crowd. Wilson storms forward and the ball comes to Hunt again. He shoots, but the ball is blocked and runs for another corner. That's three in the first five minutes. Mazurkieviez's nerves must be screaming.

But the Uruguayans have been thinking. They have begun by lavishing their attention on one part of the field only, the one they are defending. They are not stupid. They know that England must go for them, their public expects nothing else. So the Uruguayans start with ten men crowding back, just as everyone in England had been told they would. To the Uruguayan players, this is common sense, the only logical tactic.

To the English crowd, it's just not right. In fact it's almost cheating.

After ten minutes, Uruguay reveal their first attacking ploy. The sun is sinking over west London, and Uruguay are kicking towards the east. Banks in his yellow jersey must be aware of orange rays beaming low over the stadium's curving lip and into his eyes. A high centre comes over. No one in a white shirt intercepts. Rocha, the elegant one, leaps and nods the ball into the path of striker Hector Silva. He hits it at Banks, who saves as a raised linesman's flag informs the referee that Silva is offside. Two shots then loop in from forty yards. Banks swallows them. Is this as daring as Uruguay will get?

Connelly picks the ball up on the right, cuts in and shoots from a distance, but the ball flies over the bar. Barely a quarter of an hour has gone and it already appears that only long-range efforts are likely to make Mazurkieviez work. He's grabbing all the crosses with ominous ease. The Uruguayans are in no hurry. From defence, they move the ball smoothly, carefully, barely breaking sweat. Near the halfway line Stiles and Rocha get acquainted, tugging at each other's shirts. Mr Zsolt steps over and ticks them off. Stiles is used to that, in any language.

Uruguay steal forward. Julio Cortes lashes one which Banks, hurried this time, turns away for a corner-kick. Bobby Charlton is brought down. So is Bobby Moore. The England fans boo. Connelly fouls. Ball fouls. The England fans fall silent. Cortes is fouled by Moore thirty yards from the England goal and takes the free-kick himself. The flight path of the ball apes the shape of a banana and there's a collective 'oooh' of relief from the crowd as no one anticipates its swerve across the face of the England goal. Half-time comes and the players troop off, Uruguay grimly satisfied, England troubled. All around the ground, supporters hope the second half isn't going to amplify their looming sense of foreboding. They seek solace in their programmes and John Players Number 6.

What they've seen from the opposition is a display of profound, professional, negative football of a type the England team has never encountered in such undiluted form in a home fixture before. It is a kind of awakening. Ramsey's teams have been criticized for being defensive. He's a manager who prefers the specialist destroyer Stiles to, say, the tricky link-man Eastham and is prepared to do away with wingers, football's thrilling outriders, altogether. But Uruguay's method has been absolute and methodical. They have played by the safest percentages they can contrive. They have come forward only when their rearguard has been rock solid. Nine men have scurried back if ever England have looked like advancing, and if they've been beaten, they have fouled. Mazurkieviez hasn't had a shot of note to save. It isn't right. But there it is.

As the second half progresses, the mood becomes steadily more desperate. When Mazurkieviez rolls the ball out to one of his defenders, the defender just taps it back. Mazurkieviez has a look at it, runs along bouncing it, rolls it out again, gets it back again, looks at it some more. He betrays no surprise whatever that it's the same ball as before. As the ref's stopwatch tick tocks and the minutes tiptoe by, the Uruguayans defend with mounting edginess. Rather than moving the ball economically towards Cortes or the glinting Rocha, they start hoofing it, hopefully, just getting it away, as far away from their own goal as they can.

English sinews tighten. In the stands, chins drop under top hats and boaters. Union Jacks are waved with renewed desperation or not waved at all. The England clap is almost silent. Bobby Moore starts striding forward. Ball scurries. Stiles waves his arms and shouts. Hunt sweats. Greaves stalks, but there's nothing to prey on. Bobby Charlton is flummoxed. Greaves crosses and Connelly heads it, an almost unknown occurrence. The ball bobbles on top of the Uruguayan bar but the willing winger, who is roaming everywhere now, has already been flagged offside.

The game is dying. England throw themselves forward. Greaves, out wide, floats another cross over and this time there's a gap at the back. Jack Charlton, loping, has joined the attack to fill it. Unchallenged at last he meets it with his head and propels the ball past the scrambling defenders, past Mazurkieviez and past the goalpost by a foot. The final whistle blows and the Uruguayans embrace as if they've won the cup itself. But it's goalless. Even Big Jack can't argue about that.

Four

Tuesday, 12 July 1966

THE WORLD champions have entered the capital of English football, the city of Liverpool. It is not the capital because Everton FC have just won the FA Cup and Liverpool FC the League Championship, but because everyone who lives there *says* it is the capital of English football, and if you don't agree with them, you're daft. And anyway, if you think about it, Liverpool is really the capital of everything: it's the capital of stand-up comedy, the capital of poetry and, of course, the capital of rock 'n' roll. The Beatles were born there. Beat that. Where better for the great Pele to display his priceless gifts?

He's still just twenty-five, but the mantle of mystique has long ennobled the Brazilians' perfect number 10. Pelé has been part of both the previous Brazilian World Cup campaigns. In Sweden in 1958, he was a sensational seventeen-year-old who scored twice in the final against the host nation. For his first, he trapped a high ball on his thigh with his back to goal, lobbed it over his own head, swivelled and lashed it into the net before it hit the ground. Like a gunslinger. Like a magician. Like nothing you've ever seen. In 1962 a ripped muscle put him out of the competition before the quarter-final against England, but everyone has seen that goal against the Swedes replayed on television. They've heard about Pelé, read about him, seen pictures of him, and little boys in playgrounds have even pretended to *be* him.

Pelé arrives on the pitch at Goodison Park to play against Bulgaria. Fifty-three thousand people have paid over £40,000 to witness this dark, exotic superman demonstrate his ineffable brilliance. That is the legend of Pelé, part fact, part the product of ropy racial theories about the innate athletic superiority of black people compared with white, and it all thrives in the minds of opponents as well as the imaginations of fans. But those opponents also know the rest of the deal with Edson Arantes do Nascimento of Santos, the 'Saints'. They know about his steel. Pelé does not only do appalling damage to defences, he knows *how* to do it. He has a cool, calculating football mind. He works the enemy out. He's also enormously strong, five feet and eight inches of hard muscle and bone. Pelé has every weapon there is with which to hurt the other side. He can bewilder, bedazzle *and* bruise them to defeat in a few seconds of a ninety-minute game. It has become grimly apparent to opponents all over the world that the only sure way to reduce this soccer god to human proportions is to kick his body until it breaks.

The Bulgarians have detailed a player to rough the great man up. His name is Peter Zhekov, and from the moment the game begins he follows Pelé everywhere. The early skirmishes take place amid an extraordinary atmosphere. Five thousand Brazilians have made their way through the back-to-back terraced houses of this old northern European port, waving banners, playing instruments and dancing, then squeezed through the brick-and-steel entrances to the ground and set up a tremendous tumult of sound and colour in honour of the team in light-blue shorts and yellow shirts.

But most of the audience are Liverpudlians. They are of a quite different character to the Brazilians. Big ships don't steam up the River Mersey in the same numbers as when the century was young, but their legacy still lends the city its salty flavour. Even its people's nickname is derived almost literally from seafarers' mouths. Scouse is a meat and vegetable dish devoured by sailors with a savoury biscuit. Now 'scouse' means 'Liverpudlians' in general, but also the way they talk, and even their whole attitude to life. They are sceptical, acquainted with the cosmopolitan scene, and mad about football. Yet they get a big kick out of the Brazilian fans, and they've turned out in force to see their fabulous team.

On the field, the pattern unfolds. Bulgaria, white men in white kit, are able and well organized and commence with a blanket defence. The Brazilians, mostly black, caress the ball to each other, almost lovingly. Zhekov wrestles Pelé, tackling him fiercely, impeding his runs. Pelé shoves and elbows back. He is acclaimed as a great sportsman and deserves the accolade, but he has learned that he cannot survive if he gives one sign of being soft. And he can be provoked. In the Little World Cup Pelé was kicked round the field by an

Argentinian called Mesiano until, deciding enough is enough, he butted him in the face with sufficient violence to see him carried off on a stretcher with a remodelled nose.

After thirteen minutes Pelé is clattered to the ground ten feet outside the Bulgarian penalty box and lies there, grimacing as his team mates remonstrate with the referee, Kurt Tschenscher of West Germany. The crowd howls. Recovering, Pelé gets to his feet and the Bulgarians form a defensive wall. Standing in it is not a happy task. The Brazilians are famous as lethal deadball specialists. The Bulgarians cup their hands round their testicles and hope for the best. When the referee blows his whistle Pelé runs up, takes the kick with his right foot and sends the ball screaming past the defensive wall and into the body of the goalkeeper George Naidenov, from whom it cannons, still humming, into the net. It is the first goal of the 1966 World Cup. The champions Brazil are in front.

Zhekov and Pelé resume hostilities, on the ball, off the ball, pushing and tugging and nudging. Pelé is getting the better of it. He forces a good save from Naidenov, one of an increasing number. But the Bulgarians must now come out and attack. They are not without resources, and their two front-runners. George Asparuhov and Dimiter Yakimov, draw applause from the locals, who are lapping it all up. Brazil's defence is not the equal of its attack and although at half-time the Bulgarians have had the worst of it, they are not beaten yet. They have Hungary and Portugal next. If they can steal a point from this game, who knows what they might accomplish?

The second half begins. Zhekov, riled, takes to eye-balling Pelé, but to little effect. And anyway the Brazilians are not a one-man team. They are oozing with smooth operators – all, like Pelé, going under enigmatic one-word nicknames which somehow set the seal on their allure. Their left winger is Jair Ventura Filho, known as Jairzhino. They have Alcindo Martha Freitas, known just as Alcindo. And they have Manoel Francisco Santos, famous as Garrincha, the electrifying 'little bird'.

After nine minutes, the Brazilians are awarded another free kick near the Bulgarians' goal, this time maybe twenty-five yards out. Garrincha strikes it and bends it ferociously past Naidenov for Brazil's second. The goal seems to contain a sober moral for the more pragmatic coaches looking for clues to the champions' weaknesses: even if you cut them down, they still get up and score. And by the end Brazil are cruising. Pelé, running from way back, flies past tackles, swerves, changes pace and lets fly, obliging the goalkeeper to produce yet more heroics. Goalkeepers enjoy a special sympathy from Liverpool's football public. But the match ends with the champions imperious, the natives flushed, the Brazilian supporters triumphant: 'Olé Brazil!' their banners clamour. 'Avente Brazil!'

It's a bad day for Werner Leimgruber and Jakob Kuhn of Switzerland. Yesterday they arrived back at the

Hallam Tower Hotel in Sheffield after the evening curfew, and now their manager has dropped them. The pair protested that they'd lost their way while out sightseeing in the steel city. Perhaps they thought they were in the Midlands. Switzerland's opponents are West Germany, whose line-up, by contrast, is impressively complete. Their captain, Seeler, has reaffirmed his talismanic status by recovering match fitness after having an artificial achilles tendon installed. 'U-we! U-we!' chants the big West German contingent in the handsomely refurbished Hillsborough stadium.

The West German team is replete with quality and experience. Goalkeeper Hans Tilkowski and striker Sigi Held are members of the Borussia Dortmund team that beat Liverpool in the final of the European Cup Winners' Cup in May, having already knocked out the holders West Ham. The stylish and experienced full-back Karl-Heinz Schnellinger plays for Milan. Midfielder Helmut Haller plays for Bologna. Another midfield player, twenty-year-old Franz Beckenbauer of Bayern Munich, is reckoned to be brimming with promise. Manager Helmut Schoen is as meticulous as England's Ramsey. No one will take liberties with his team.

The World Cup seems to have prompted visiting spectators to indulge in shameless displays of self-parody. The small band of Swiss make a spectacle of themselves by rattling cow bells, the staple souvenir of their burgeoning domestic tourist trade. But they are silenced after a quarter of an hour. Held, nimble and mobile, nips past two defenders on the left and crosses the ball to Seeler. The tough man with the captain's armband turns a shot against the Swiss goalkeeper Charles Elsener. Held, following up, pockets the rebound.

Five minutes later the blond, chunky Haller collects a stray ball, beats one man and places his shot in the furthest corner of the net. The contest becomes an execution. As half-time approaches, Beckenbauer glides smoothly upfield. He cuts a slight figure, still adolescent but immensely poised under black curly hair. Seeler, never resting, is in space to receive a pass and gives the ball back to his provider, who continues his advance. The West German fans' urgings soar to a climax as Beckenbauer breaches the Swiss line and increases the lead to three. The Swiss head for the dressing room, helpless, already destroyed.

In the second half, the Germans are almost dismissive. Beckenbauer dribbles around two Swiss defenders, invites Elsener to dispossess him, withdraws the invitation and neatly plants his second. Seeler is baulked in the penalty box and referee Hugh Phillips of Scotland awards a penalty. Haller is the man to take it. He runs up, but, just at the point of drawing back his shooting boot, hesitates in mid-stride. Elsener, anticipating, dives. Haller, smiling inside, strikes the ball inside the opposite post to the one the goalkeeper has headed for. Five–nil.

Their business done, the West Germans head back to their hotel in the Derbyshire Peaks, put their feet up and consider the view from the top of Group Two.

*

The *Official Handbook* of the 1966 World Cup sings the praises of Middlesbrough in English, German, Spanish and French. It describes a district of Yorkshire known as Teesside, home of 400,000 people blessed with iron, steel and chemical plants, docks and riverside wharfs, modern offices and 'a thriving air of prosperity'. It highlights, too, the colourful displays of flowers and plants which have made Middlesbrough the only industrial town to reach the finals of the Britain in Bloom competition. Even the weather is recommended: Middlesbrough boasts one of the lowest annual rates of rainfall in the country.

This brightness and enterprise is personified by Charlie Amer, a member of Middlesbrough FC's board and an energetic local businessman. He has his work cut out on the football front because Middlesbrough have just been relegated to Division Three for the first time in their history. But being named a World Cup venue (thanks to Newcastle United's local difficulties) has proved an opportunity to make improvements to the Ayresome Park ground, including putting a roof over the east-end terrace. Of course, it would all have been much better if there were some fancier teams in Group Four to cheer up a depressed local soccer clientele. Nonetheless, Denis Howell has made Middlesbrough his first port of call on his journey round the country to host government receptions for the visiting-team parties. It's a big day at Ayresome Park.

Howell arrives in Middlesbrough in plenty of time to check in to his hotel – which happens to be owned by Charlie Amer – and get to the match between the

USSR and North Korea which kicks off later in the evening. On a whim, he asks his driver to take a detour to Ayresome Park to peruse the facilities provided for the foreign dignitaries. His car pulls up outside the main entrance next to a lorry, from the back of which a set of wooden stairs is being lifted. Men in overalls proceed to push these steps into position enabling the reception area to be reached without recourse to a labyrinth of internal corridors. Then, at the top of the steps, Charlie Amer appears. He has a roll of red carpet, a hammer and a box of tacks. Howell heads for his hotel hoping for the best.

Howell has managed to subdue the splutters of political disapproval provoked by North Korea's presence. He has been instrumental in the see-no-evil understanding with the Foreign Office which has enabled the North Korean flag to be flown. The problem of the anthem has been solved thanks to an agreement with Sir Stanley Rous that, apart from the opening match and the final, no national anthems at all will be played. This is principally because neither Howell, Rous nor anyone else can stand them. The only remaining source of embarrassment is the North Koreans' names. Like the Brazilians, their official monikers are three-part epics: Han Bong Zin, Kang Ryong Woon, Pak Doo Ik. Unlike the Brazilians, they do not dispense with these in favour of shortened versions or resonant invented nicknames for common usage. So how should Pak Doo Ik be called for shorthand? 'Pak', 'Doo' or just plain 'Ik'?

Such matters are a source of confusion and amusement to the unspectacular crowd of 23,000 which turns up to watch representatives of the Soviet Threat and the Mysterious East try to outdo each other beneath advertising hoardings for Newcastle Brown Ale. Both sides are unknown quantities, although in different ways. The Soviet Union – or the 'Russians' as everyone insists on calling them – have qualified easily, winning all their matches against Denmark and Wales, except the second against the latter in Cardiff when they were already assured of their place. Everyone agrees that they will be disciplined and efficient, but short of flair. But that's all anyone in England ever says about Soviet football teams or, for that matter, Soviet goats, fish or tea cosies. They are 'Russians', after all.

As for the North Koreans, no one has much of a clue because no one has seen them play except Sir Stanley Rous. He's witnessed their progress through qualifying Group Sixteen, which included no other nation except Australia, because everybody else in Africa and Asia – South Korea, Ghana, Guinea, Cameroon, Sudan, Algeria, Nigeria, Tunisia, Liberia, Senegal, Morocco, Mali, Ethiopia, Gabon, Libya and the United Arab Republic – boycotted it. They pulled out because the fact that they had all been squashed into the group meant that only one of them could be represented in the final series games. The two Group Sixteen fixtures were played within three days of each other on the unlikely neutral territory of Phnom Penh, Cambodia, in front of impressive crowds of 48,000 and 40,000. The North Koreans won both, easily. But that, as far as the West is concerned, represents their entire competitive international record. It isn't much to go on.

However, the North Koreans do have one great advantage. Because they are novel, small and expected to get slaughtered, the Ayresome Park regulars are automatically on their side. And when the game kicks off, the locals launch into a chant: 'KO-RE-A! KO-RE-A!' By contrast, the only Soviet player who might enjoy the crowd's recognition and affection is its charismatic goalkeeper, Lev Yashin. But Yashin is injured and can't play.

The North Koreans set about their task busily. In midfield Im Seung Hwi and Pak Seung Zin interpass and fizz about. In attack Pak Doo Ik embarks on a discouraging quest to unsettle Murtaz Khurtsilava, a large Soviet defender. For half an hour their endeavour secures their place in the Teessiders' hearts as the lovable underdogs, the wonderful 'Wongs'. But the Soviets are untroubled. And on the half-hour Eduard Malofeev, a strapping striker, strokes a pass beyond the lone defender on the North Korean goal-line after goalkeeper Li Chan Myung has stranded himself out of position. Straight after the kick-off North Korea lose possession. The ball comes to Anatoliy Banishevskiy, who cuts in from the right and lashes in a second. The Koreans have been crushed inside a minute. They struggle through to half-time. 'Don't Be Vague, Ask for Haig' suggests a Scotch whisky advertisement mounted on the front of one of Ayresome's renovated stands. The North Koreans could do with some.

For the USSR, the second half is a canter. Again, the North Koreans start by going at them with gusto. Again the Middlesbrough crowd roars them on. Again, they fail to threaten. Then, in the seventy-eighth minute, Iosif Sabo, the Soviets' best player, steers a fine pass into Malofeev's path. He converts the chance thunderously. The Soviets depart Ayresome Park without a worry, except for a caution for Khurtsilava, booked for violent play. Already, it is a physical tournament. The North Koreans leave to affectionate applause, but they look like boys against giants.

Five

Wednesday, 13 July 1966

EUSEBIO DA Silva Ferreira was born in Lourenço Marques, Portuguese East Africa, in 1942, and lived in the part of the city to which native subjects were consigned by the colonial power. Old photos of his home show a corrugated iron shack. As a boy he fell in love with football and played in the street with a ball made from paper, rags and stockings. And when he was eleven, he and his friends formed a team. They called themselves The Brazilians, and took to adopting the names of the great Brazilian players, fellow men of colour who spoke the same language as they did and played the game the heroic way.

Eusebio went on to play for the Lourenço Marques Sporting Club, an established feeder team for the great football powers in Portugal, and when he was eighteen he received a telephone call from the Benfica club in Lisbon, telling him to get on the next plane over. Eusebio – by then known only by that single name – survived the transition from Africa to Europe with distinction, and when he was twenty he took part in the 1962 European Cup final against Real Madrid, helping Benfica win by five goals to three, getting two of them himself and swapping shirts with the great Hungarian Ferenc Puskas (who got all of Real's goals) at the end. By then Eusebio had played his first game at Wembley, against England in a qualifying match for the 1962 World Cup. Portugal lost, two–nil. He returned in October 1963 as a member of the Rest of the World team which played England. Again he was on the losing side, and got carried off after a tackle with Maurice Norman of Tottenham Hotspur, who was Alf Ramsey's choice of centre-half at that time. But despite these reverses, Eusebio loved the ugly old stadium. He wanted more.

Now he is twenty-four and has spent the last few days lodging at the Stannylands hotel in Wilmslow, not far from Manchester. His companions have been the rest of the Portuguese national team, all complaining about the cold. And the press have been with them everywhere: when they got off the plane at Manchester airport; when they went training at the ground of nearby Cheadle Rovers; when they took over the hotel kitchen to make their own *bacalhuazada*, a hot codfish stew with plenty of peppers. Chief cook is José Augusto, regular choice for the midfield. Eusebio wore the chef's hat. The photographers liked that.

This Eusebio is something special, a 'black panther' they are calling him, from the African land that is now popularly known as Mozambique. He is fast, smooth and strong, with a ferocious scoring shot in his right foot. Beginning with comparisons between Eusebio and Pelé, the Portuguese, playing in their first World Cup final series, are seen as a kind of junior Brazil: a blend of Latin and magical black men, gifted, explosive, full of trickery and style.

Their first opponents are Hungary, whom they meet at Old Trafford, Manchester United's field of dreams. The Hungarians bring their own reputation for artistry and flair. The legends of 1953 – Puskas, Kocsis, Hidegkuti – who demolished England at Wembley have all hung their boots up now, but there are new stars to replace them: Janos Farkas, Florian Albert, the winger Ferenc Bene. Under grey skies before 37,000, the game kicks off and Eusebio makes the sign of the cross on his chest, requesting the blessing of God. He wears number 13 for good luck.

It pays off. After one minute Hungarian goalkeeper Antal Szentmihalyi is injured. After two minutes Portugal win a corner on the left and the Hungarians urgently organize themselves to deal with the threat of the enormous Benfica centre-forward José Torres. The ball arcs over. Everybody misses it except José Augusto, also of Benfica, who nods it into the net. Maybe it was the Almighty, answering Eusebio's prayer. Maybe it was the peppered codfish.

For the next twenty minutes, the Hungarians look half lost, the Portuguese hugely fluent. All the training, all the planning, all the pre-match nerves and concentration. All the talent on both sides. And suddenly only one of the two teams is functioning as it hoped. Portugal threaten. Their captain Mario Coluna, yet another Benfica player (and also from Mozambique), is the brains of their midfield. Eusebio is everywhere. Hungary can only hang on and hope their muse will appear from somewhere. Their defenders tackle desperately. There's a high ball, Eusebio leaps, Szentmihalyi, still struggling, lunges. Missing his target, he punches Eusebio above the left eye and fells him. Number 13 is taken from the field and fitted with a bandage. By the time he returns, just before the interval, the Hungarians have achieved some sort of purchase on the game. And, as the second half starts, they attack. Albert looks slippery, Bene quick. Then Joaquim Carvalho, the Portuguese goalie, endures a painful moment of truth. He is a big man in a thick goalie's sweater and a peaked tweed cap: Manchester weather can make a custodian shiver. He moves forward to claim a Hungarian centre but fails to grab it as Albert challenges. The loose ball falls to Bene, who drives it home. One-all. Hungary are back from the half-dead. But not for long. This time it's Szentimihalyi who makes a mistake between the sticks. Torres, much more than a lumbering lighthouse, lobs a limp centre towards him. The keeper goes to catch it, misses, it bounces off his chest and there again is the head of happy José Augusto. Two–one. Then, with the Welsh referee Leo Callaghan looking at his watch, Eusebio, who's played superbly, takes a corner, swerving the ball towards the furthest post. Torres towers, and Portugal clinch it.

Eusebio, beaming sweetly, leaves the field to look for an ice pack.

The new *International Football Book* contains an article by the expensive Luis Suarez. He philosophizes on the importance of intuition: 'It is the instinctive action,' he writes – or his hired ghost does, anyway – 'which makes effective the general scheme of the team. Considered tactics, however efficient, can be read and countered unless they have a great deal of novelty. But who can foresee the instinctive action, the unexpected moment of magic which materializes out of an otherwise dead situation to win a game?'

Suarez has already helped Internazionale win the European Cup in 1965. He is wealthy, a winner, and his mugshots give him the gleaming look of a Latin movie star. Now he is at Villa Park to help Spain improve on their curiously poor record in the World Cup. They have only once reached the last four, in 1950, and they have scraped through the qualifiers this time, beating their sole opponents, the Republic of Ireland (Syria, originally the third team in their qualifying group, withdrew), by the odd goal in a play-off in Paris. But Suarez is special and Spain have travelled hopefully from Sutton Coldfield into England's second city to meet the mean men of Argentina.

In English eyes Argentina are the ultimate 'South Americans', the personification of footballing profanity. Yet they are cuter than they've been billed, and their preparation has shown a striking absence of the cynical calculation said to inform their style of play. There's been a sudden change of manager with Juan Carlos Lorenzo, who did the job in Chile, being recalled. They've also brought back to their squad two players from the famous River Plate club of Buenos Aires who had been reduced to turning out for the reserves. One is Ermindo Onega, a prompting inside-forward, loaded with flair. The other is striker Luis Artime, nicknamed the 'Handsome One'.

Both are picked to play against the Spanish and are led on to the field by captain Antonio Rattin, a tall midfield generalissimo blessed with rich footballing gifts. After Pelé nutted his Argentine tormentor during the 1964 Little World Cup, Rattin came on as substitute and methodically marked the Brazilian genius out of the rest of the game. Rattin, it is said, is a millionaire and owns a cork forest. He has the manner of an aristocrat – maybe Rattin was born to wealth. The 48,000 crowd soon gathers that impression as play gets under way. Rattin appears to be running the game except that he doesn't actually *run* at all. He trots. He may occasionally canter. Anything more taxing would be undignified.

At first, all eyes are on Suarez, who makes a couple of early runs at the men in pale-blue-and-white striped shirts. Both times he is clattered to the ground. But Argentina do not only repulse with pragmatic breaches of the law. This is just one of the cruder aspects of a more ingenious system. At the very back they employ Roberto Perfumo as a sweeper, a free man who checks any impertinent enemy incursions through his back line or Rattin's miserly midfield. These defensive units erect an imaginary barrier across the pitch about thirty yards from their own goal and seek to smother all who try to cross it. But they also use this platform as a springboard. They have two skilled and pacey full-backs who overlap from the back, they have a fleet little winger called

76

Oscar Mas, they have Onega and they have the Handsome One.

Spain play in a similar fashion, but they are not as good at it and Suarez can summon no instinctive action with which to confound Argentina's considered tactics. Argentina, though, break forward frequently. In the second half they take the lead. Artime releases link man Jorge Solari, who runs and centres back towards Artime, who has eluded all markers at the far post. He accepts the chance expertly. Already knowing that penetrating Argentina is like picking locks at Fort Knox, the Spanish throw themselves boldly forward and José Martinez heads an equalizer in his first international match. But, with ten minutes left, Perfumo places a pass into the path of Artime, who controls it without apparent effort and smashes the winning goal. Spain one, the Handsome One two.

When the Italians stepped off their aircraft in London they looked every inch what they are: lean, loaded and fabulously chic. Other teams have seemed discomfited by having to tuck themselves into regulation suits. But the Italians looked svelte in theirs. Most slick of all, they wore mid-blue shirts with big, broad collars... *and no ties.* This sort of thing is not common in Sunderland, where the Italians' first match in Group Four takes place. Sunderland is shipbuilding country, and Roker Park, the ground of its local football club, is not celebrated as a seedbed of sartorial innovation.

Not that the town by the River Wear has skimped

on its World Cup effort. Two Information Centres have been set up to cater to the needs of visitors. All letters passing through the Sunderland General Post Office are franked with the legend: 'World Cup Competition – Sunderland, July 13th-23rd'. Three hundred sets of special presentation glasses have been made, engraved with scenes of Sunderland. Four hundred places of accommodation have been booked by visiting Italians. Today, another five thousand have descended, unannounced. The local press and the BBC have put out emergency appeals. Most of the Mediterranean visitors are now wedged into Roker waving banners saying 'Forza!' and chanting 'IT-AL-IA! IT-AL-IA!' They make up about one-sixth of the crowd. Football mad.

Their opponents are Chile, who have arrived more in hope than expectation having scrambled through their qualifying group after a play-off against Ecuador. More unused than most to northern European conditions, they look unlikely to prosper against either today's opponents or the Soviets. But neither side can be entirely happy about the Sunderland weather. Here we are in midsummer and it's poured for two hours before kick-off. The conditions seem to confirm the wisdom of the Italians, wearing their famous blue shirts, in making caution their watchword for this, their opening game. It is not unusual for Italian managers to have their critics back home, but Edmondo Fabbri has more than most, and any slip-up in this encounter is unthinkable. He's picked Sandro Salvadore, Giovanni Lodetti and Tarcisio Burgnich at the heart of an elaborate defence, along with Internazionale's Giacinto Facchetti, a Ferrari of a full-back. Milan's dark and deluxe Gianni Rivera is in midfield and another Inter man, Sandro Mazzola, is in attack. It is a polished line-up, potentially brilliant. But a quiet, clinical victory will suit Fabbri just fine.

His team take a huge step towards that within ten minutes. Midfielder Giacomo Bulgarelli stops a Chilean attack in its tracks and releases winger Paolo Barison, whose shot is only parried by the Chilean keeper. Mazzola, following up, slides in to punish the error. The Italians sustain their superiority with ease, though without managing to add to their score. In the second half Bulgarelli is reduced to limping pace, but Chile's striker Armando Tobar has to leave the field entirely. It's now ten-and-a-half men versus ten. Two minutes from the end, Barison scores a second goal. The Italians have cruised it. They meet the Soviet Union next.

At Wembley Stadium Alf Ramsey, his assistants and the England squad sit in the stand hoping not to be impressed by either Mexico or France. A nice, drab draw will do the trick, leaving all four teams in Group One level on points and on goal average. It will be almost like starting all over again and England won't mind that in the slightest.

Still, they've cheered up quite a bit since the worrying draw with Uruguay two nights ago. Some of the players couldn't get off the pitch fast enough after the final whistle went. Four of them bolted into the dressing room without waiting for a second playing of the national anthem as they were supposed to, a point that did not go unnoticed by some of the more eagle-eyes pressmen present. But as the England players stripped glumly for their bath, Ramsey had put the evening's result into perspective: Banks had had just two shots of consequence to deal with and better luck might have put England on the score-sheet; defeat, on the other hand, would have been disastrous, and that had been avoided. A draw against the toughest opposition in Group One kept them right in contention for the quarters. Then Ramsey went up the little spiral staircase at the back of the England dressing room to give his post-match television interview to David Coleman of the BBC. He told Coleman he was satisfied with the England performance and that he still believed England would win the World Cup. He didn't add, 'So sod the lot of you,' but it is possible that he thought it.

The next day, the England party ignored the morning papers, some of which were proclaiming a national humiliation, and went on a day trip. Their destination was the Pinewood film studios and their hosts were a galaxy of stars. Lunch was laid on and everyone had a few drinks. Yul Brynner talked about training horses on the Russian steppes. Norman Wisdom did an imitation of a one-man football team, which tickled the England lads pink. They watched Sean Connery shooting scenes for the latest James Bond movie, and at the end of the afternoon Ramsey made a short speech, thanking Connery (despite his being a Scotsman) for his hospitality on behalf of the England party. To the considerable but concealed amusement of all present, Ramsey pronounced the actor's first name 'Seen', as it is spelt, prompting Jimmy Greaves to remark to his mate Bobby Moore, 'That was the funniest thing I've ever Sean or heard.' Essex lads Greaves and Moore found particular amusement in Ramsey's social affectations and comprehensive squareness.

The Pinewood trip did the trick. It relaxed the England players. And today it is back to training with a refreshed sense of purpose and, in some cases, a growing anxiety about what changes Ramsey will make for the next game. After the moral defeat against Uruguay, there will surely have to be some.

But before that come the frustrations of spectating. The World Cup Organization's ticket sales strategy seems vindicated by the Wembley scene. The stadium is far from full, but a house of nearly 70,000 is not bad, especially when one of the teams comes from Central America and has no great football tradition. That said, it is the Mexican fans who are making the most memorable racket. From beneath the brims of their sombreros they set up their chant of 'MEH-I-CO! MEH-I-CO!' and sustain it for long periods. It is as well that they are introducing themselves with such enthusiasm, because their team is an unknown quantity. The French, by contrast, are known well, largely for their recent decline. Where England have grown in strength since being walloped by them in Paris at the very start of Ramsey's managerial reign, the French have slithered towards mediocrity.

They certainly don't frighten the Mexicans, who advance with blithe optimism, feeding their charismatic centre-forward Enrique Borja copiously and confusing the French defence with their energy and speed. Just before half-time Borja mishits a shot at the French goal, but has enough time for another go and spoils French keeper Marcel Aubour's day. Shaken, the French pull themselves together after the break. Their midfield is still disjointed and the highly rated Nestor Combin (who was born in Argentina) is a big disappointment. But Gerard Hausser equalizes with a long shot that goes in off a post. The game is an entertaining muddle, littered with mistakes. The French look short on conviction, the Mexicans lively but naive. For the England party in the stand, though, the main thing is the result. One–all. And with that happy scoreline delivered as if in answer to their prayers, they leave for Hendon Hall with every reason for good cheer.

Six

Friday, 15 July 1966

OUT AT Lymm on the Cheshire coast, the Brazilians' preparations for their second Group Three match have not been going smoothly. Manager Vincente Feola, a chubby man with a penchant for tiny, horn-rimmed sunglasses, has problems made more awkward by the fact that most are not of his own creation. For example, Feola cannot be blamed for the flotilla of soccer boffins, psychologists and moral protectors who are attached to the Brazilian camp and with whose largely unwanted advice he is obliged to contend. His players care for these interfering people still less than Feola does. It is rumoured that the Beatles have offered to play a private show for the team, but that this had been declined for fear of the lovable moptops corrupting the innocent young Brazilians with their sinful rhythms and likely enthusiasm for mind-expanding drugs.

The irony is that many of the Brazilians are, in football terms, very far from young. The striking thing about Feola's squad is that he has kept faith with many of the stars of the last two World Cup campaigns, despite their being (unlike Pelé) either clearly past their prime, or able to reach their former glorious heights only intermittently. Garrincha and the elegant full-back Djalma Santos are the most prominent examples. They don't mend as quickly as they used to and this is already a World Cup heavy with physical punishment. That opening match against Bulgaria was a rough, tough encounter and it has taken its toll most dispiritingly on Pelé. Surrounded, kicked and tripped by desperate defenders every time the ball went near him, he came off battered and bruised and has been declared unfit for the match against Hungary. Yet despite the Bulgarians – in particular Zhekov – dispensing this treatment throughout the whole of the ninety minutes, not one of them was sent off or even booked.

There has been much talk before the tournament about the tendency of European and South American officials to interpret the laws of the game differently, and the South American teams were not reassured by the heavy European bias in the thirty-one referees chosen by FIFA for the World Cup, of whom seven are Englishmen. The referee for the game against Hungary is one of these Englishmen, Kenneth Dagnall, and so is one of the linesmen, Kevin Howley. The other is Arturo Yamasaki from Peru.

The Brazilians might also have some historic reason for apprehension about today's opponents. The Hungarians were the last team to beat Brazil in a World Cup match. As a precedent it is not auspicious. The sides met in a quarter-final in Switzerland in 1954. The great Hungarians (though without the injured Puskas) won four–two, but if the scoreline suggests an elevating spectacle, the reality was rather different. A punch-up on the pitch resulted in one player from each side being sent off, and a second Brazilian followed for foul play. After the match, the two teams resumed hostilities in the Hungarians' dressing room. The occasion has gone down in history as the Battle of Berne. The referee was an Englishman, Arthur Ellis. He was one of the few to survive with his reputation unsullied, though not in the eyes of partisan Brazilians.

The 1966 Hungarians are not the equal of their illustrious forebears. They are, however, talented and frustrated. Bad luck played its part in their defeat against Portugal, but they are displeased with themselves for their incoherence during the first third of the match. They know, too, that a good result today is vital if they are to sustain realistic hopes of proceeding to the second phase. They ought to beat Bulgaria in their final group game. But that future fixture may be academic if they fail to beat Brazil first. For Hungary, in their wine-red shirts, it's time to do or die. They have made three changes from the Portugal game, which include the replacement of the ill-starred Szentmihalyi in goal by Jozsef Gelei. The Brazilians have brought in Gerson (Gerson Oliveira Nunes) for Denilson and Tostao (Eduardo Gonçalves Andrade) for Pelé. The Merseyside weather threatens with storm clouds and gusting wind, but 57,000 people pack into Goodison Park. They have come for poetry. They get some.

From the kick-off Brazil coax the ball purposefully across the midfield and Gelei is required to execute a giant leap towards the left-hand corner of his goal, edging a ferocious shot from thirty yards over the crossbar with tingling fingertips. But Hungary go straight back down the field, forcing goalkeeper Gylmar to scramble a low shot round the post. All this in the first two minutes. Then Bene raids down the right. He's a tiny, wiry man with fine, fair hair and legs that move so fast they seem almost to blur like those of a cartoon mouse evading the swipes of an angry cat. He's a real dasher. He leaves one defender stuck in mid-plod on the corner of the Brazilian box. Another looms, and Bene swerves to his left with such startling suddenness that the defender, two yards from his own goal, backs off in confusion. Bene, stealing an upward glance, spots a slot between the defender and the frantic, advancing Gylmar. With a sharp swing of his left foot, he propels the ball straight through it, along the ground, inside the post and into the net.

On the terraces and in the stands there's an eruption of delight which engulfs the drums and percussion of the Brazilian contingent and reduces them to silence. The Liverpool neutrals are wowed, knocked out. This is what they've paid their money for. This is what the capital city of English football expects. Now they're rooting for the underdogs, who have shown they know how to bite.

The Brazilians respond. In the fifteenth minute, surging forward, they are awarded a free kick twenty-five yards from Gelei's goal. The Hungarians construct a defensive wall and sundry Brazilians hover round its edges. The kick is taken by the big centre-half Lima. It crashes against the wall, ricochets from body to body and falls for the lurking Tostao, who slams the stray ball into the top corner with his left foot, leaving Gelei grasping vainly at its slipstream. It's one–all at half-time. They have been pressed into making one desperate goal-line clearance, but the Hungarians look the more fluent, the more complete. Brazil are performing in patches. Garrincha has hardly been seen.

As the teams resume it seems as if some special music must be playing in the souls of the Hungarians. From the opening moments, their pitch is perfect. The conductor of the orchestra is Florian Albert, wearing 9, the pride of Budapest. Albert roams and ravages. He drops deep to receive the ball and floats through the open spaces in the heart of Brazil's midfield. They have no mechanism for subduing him as the Argentinians might have had, no one to harass or pursue him, no spoilsport Nobby Stiles.

It takes them an almost unreal twenty minutes of the second forty-five, but the Hungarians finally seize the lead they deserve. Albert feeds Bene with a perfect first-time pass. Bene crosses early, fast and low. He's seen Janos Farkas, number 10, arriving in the penalty area at full steam, his socks rumpled around his ankles, screaming for a pass. Bene's cross comes to Farkas at just below knee height. This ought to make it awkward, but Farkas does not break stride. As he intercepts the flight of the ball, he bends his body over it and cracks it straight past Gylmar like a bullet from a gun.

Oh joy! Everybody in the crowd with the slightest understanding of the finer arts of football knows that they have seen a rare and special sight. Anyone who's ever played a scratch game in the park knows how very hard it is to execute a move like that, a perfect interchange of passes, three minds locked on the same wavelength, a co-ordinated act of creation, requiring supreme confidence and daring. The crowd basks: 'Easy! Easy!'

The champions are sinking. Alcindo is limping on the touchline, diminishing still further Brazil's capacity to hit back. The defence looks aged and pedestrian. The crowd are calling the name of Albert. He has the ball again, just inside his own half. He sways between two tacklers and he's away, smooth and coasting like a racing yacht in full sail. He looks up, finds Bene, and the little winger whisks round two defenders, leaving them scrambled in his wake. One, Altair, hangs a leg out and Bene crashes down. Kenneth Dagnall gives a penalty. The Hungarian captain, Kalman Meszoly, steps up to take it. He hits it low to Gylmar's right and the keeper hardly has time to shape before the ball crosses his line.

It's over now, but Hungary still fly into the attack. There are near-misses and Farkas has a second goal disallowed for offside. Meszoly gets injured and has to leave the field, but he's arguing with his trainer on the touchline, frantic to return to the action. The trainer remonstrates, but the captain gets his way. He plays out the last few minutes with his left arm in a sling. As the final whistle blows, the Goodison crowd renews its call of 'Albert! Albert! Albert!', pronouncing the *t* at the end of his name with the full scouse rasp, even though in Hungary that last letter is silent. But the number 9 knows exactly who they're talking to, and he is the last to leave the field, gulping and dousing himself from a soda-water siphon and waving his thanks to these most discriminating Englishmen who don't bestow their favours on just any Fancy Dan.

On the way out, one adult spectator says to his eleven-year-old son that he's been privileged to see two great Alberts at Goodison Park now: Florian from Budapest, and Albert Dunlop, the old Everton goalkeeper. Back-handed humour is, perhaps, the greatest Liverpool tribute, and the 1966 World Cup has just seen its first great match.

At the Hendon Hall hotel, the England players have been whiling away the last evening before meeting Mexico, some of them worried half to death about whether or not they'll be playing. Otherwise, it's all a bit boring, really, but at least there's football on telly. The BBC has fixed up a special television which enables them to watch any of the matches played on any day, not just the one being beamed to the public at large. Today, Kenneth Wolstenholme has gone up to Goodison for the evening's main attraction and been as delighted by Florian Albert as the fans: 'Look at this boy, he's a charmer.' Nicely put.

Alternatively, there's Switzerland versus Spain at Hillsborough. Although both sides have lost their opening games, neither are yet eliminated and either could be England's opponents if they reach the quarter-final. The Spanish start the match in their great World Cup tradition – poorly. Switzerland have reinstated Kuhn and Leimgruber following their costly sightseeing mis-judgement and have made five other changes after their drubbing by the West Germans. At first, it works well for them. In the first half, they cream the Spaniards, and their striker René-Pierre Quentin side-foots an easy opener. In goal, Elsener is a virtual spectator.

But in the second half the Swiss, inexplicably, fall apart, while the Spanish apply themselves to their uphill task with spirit. On the left flank is Francisco Gento, a veteran of the great Real Madrid team which dominated the European Cup in the second half of the 1950s and which has won it again in 1966. Gento looks a little porky in his twilight years. But after a half-time breather he zips into his stride. Suarez looks more lively too. The tide finally turns when Manuel Sanchis, the Spanish defender, is allowed to make forty yards on his own without a single Swiss player offering a tackle. Suddenly within sight of goal, he dinks it insouciantly over Els-ener to equalize. Quentin has a goal disallowed soon after, then Gento responds by outstripping the Swiss defence and crossing for Amaro Amancio, another Real star, to dive and head a pearler to win the match. For the moment, Spain are level with West Germany and Argentina on points. They can still get through. The Swiss, though, are finished.

Meanwhile, at Ayresome Park, details have begun emerging of the North Koreans' diet. The St George Hotel at the airport near Darlington has never served breakfasts quite like it: rice, beef and noodle soup, cabbage, cucumber and onions with soya sauce, tomatoes, beef and eggs, apples, bread and butter, and coffee. They might only be little fellows, but even after that they still had room for lunch: rice, chicken, fish, eggs, apples, cucumber, carrots, pork and mushrooms, plus chocolate for dessert and cider and soda-water to wash it down. Good grief. There has also been clarification over the correct abbreviation of names. The BBC's commentator for most of Group Four matches is a promising young broadcaster called Frank Bough. A visit to the North Korean manager has revealed that all three parts of the North Koreans' names should be used. Lesser men might have crumbled. But Bough has risen to the challenge. And just as well: the BBC expects no less.

There is a poor crowd of 16,000 for the North Koreans' second appearance at Ayresome Park, but almost all of it is rooting for the unfancied orientals. Chile are their opponents, minus the injured Tobar from their encounter with Italy. The opening half-hour is error-strewn to the point of absurdity. Defenders flail, strikers miss the target. Thrown into a spin, North Korean defender Lim Zoong Sun pulls down Pedro Araya, the most dangerous of the Chileans, who are getting well on top. Ruben Marcos converts the penalty.

It looks like curtains for the North Koreans as they trot out under an overcast sky for the second half. But they rally, roared on again by the men of Middlesbrough in their flat working-men's caps. Delightedly, the locals have taken to referring to the North Koreans as 'we' and 'us'. But the pressure on the Chilean goal is erratic and imperfectly applied and as the game

approaches its conclusion the disappointing scoreline
stays the same. Two minutes to go, and there's a ruck
of Chilean defenders blocking the way to their goal.
Pak Seung Zin lets fly. The ball flashes through the ruck.
It's there! Two minutes to go, and North Korea have
scored their first goal, got their first point and kept their
World Cup hopes alive. At the final whistle an enormous
English sailor in full navy rig climbs over the barrier
and embraces the nearest North Korean. The photographers eat it up. Now, all North Korea have to do is
beat the Italians and hope for the best.

About 150,000 people are at World Cup matches
tonight. None are more intent on what they are seeing
than Alf Ramsey at the White City stadium where Uruguay play France. In London, the weather is worse than
anywhere else where games are being played. It's raining
and the sky is so overcast that the stadium floodlights
are switched on from the kick-off. The white Slazenger
ball catches their beams as it skids across the sopping
turf, which more usually provides a surface for javelin
throwers and show jumpers. Ramsey is there without
his players this time. He is especially keen to get more
of a measure of the French.

They seem strengthened this evening by the selection
of Jacques Simon, a busy, clever midfield player who's
in in place of Combin, and the French begin by going
forward with a will. It may not be pleasing for Ramsey
to see that their forwards Hausser and Yves Herbet
enjoy more success against the Uruguayan defence in

the first few minutes than England did in the entire opening game. And when Herbet races through and is levelled in the penalty area, Hector de Bourgoing puts France ahead from the spot.

The early goal releases the match's potential for commitment and drama. The Uruguayans cannot possibly sit back on a one-goal deficit, for if they lose they are in peril and their fate will partly lie in the outcome of other matches. So at last they become more expansive. Adventuring into the French penalty area, they thread the ball neatly to Rocha, who strikes it cleanly home. Six minutes after that, they score again. This time it's the energetic Cortes who does the job from a narrow angle. At two–one up, they revert to type. Hausser hits the bar in the second half, but Mazurkieviez, the 'Grey Ghost', is little troubled. As against England, Uruguay play remorselessly within themselves. A disgusted Simon spits at the Czechoslovakian referee on his way off and is booked for his trouble.

Alf Ramsey departs more demurely. The mathematics of Group One now make it likely that Uruguay will qualify while the thin hopes of France rest initially on England first failing to beat Mexico at Wembley. Ramsey heads back to the Hendon Hall, where his players should be thinking about getting ready for bed. In the morning, he'll let them know which ones are playing and on which others he has decided to inflict one of the biggest disappointments of their careers.

Seven

Saturday, 16 July 1966

CONNELLY IS out. Ball is out.

Ramsey tells them in the morning and both are broken up.

On the team coach heading for Wembley Ramsey has a private word with Connelly, whose unhappiness is etched deep in his face. If they had won against Uruguay, he says, he would have selected the same side. But they didn't, so someone else must have their chance. It's cruel news for Connelly. He's done so well, come so far from being a joiner in a coalmine to turning out for Manchester United alongside Charlton, Denis Law and Georgie Best. He's a fine player: he can go by them on the outside, left or right, he can cut in and score, he's brave. After his frustrations in Chile in 1962 he's forced his way back into Ramsey's England set-up and it looked like it might be to stay. He'd walked out at Wembley on Monday, stood for the national anthem, met the Queen, felt the lump rise in his throat. Then he'd tried his heart out against that miserly defence. He'd even headed one against the bar. Now this.

Ball is a picture of heartache. He shares with Stiles at Hendon Hall – Ramsey decides the pairings – in the top room and they get on like a house on fire. They're the rebels, they gee each other up, they've got things to prove. At bedtime Stiles tells 'little Bally' that they're gonna win this World Cup, don't you worry, you'll be a hero, my old mate. Bally likes all that. He likes Ramsey too, but not just at this moment. Ball doesn't exactly know why he's been demoted. He got a knock against Uruguay, maybe that's a factor. But you don't question Ramsey's decisions, you just accept them quietly. And little Bally is very, very quiet.

Terry Paine is in. Martin Peters is in.

Paine's job will be to pull the Mexicans apart down the right-hand side. His club Southampton, just promoted, was in the Second Division when Ramsey first picked him. He's experienced, sturdy, dark-haired and a ball-player who's enjoyed a couple of purple patches in the England team. He got a goal against the Rest of the World in 1963 and a hat-trick in the next England game when they beat Northern Ireland eight-three, the first Wembley match played under floodlights. He saw off the challenge of Peter Thompson for the number 7 shirt, but began losing out to Ball as Ramsey started experimenting with 4–3–3. Now, suddenly, he's back in favour. It's a dream.

So what about Peters, now favoured for the left of midfield? It will only be his second cap and, although he's an impressive West Ham regular, he remains oddly unknown. He's from Plaistow, east London, aged twenty-two, six feet tall, looks more scrawny than his eleven stone ten pounds. The England wags call him the Duke of Kent, because there's a trace of a likeness.

As a player, though, Peters isn't very much like anyone else. It took Ron Greenwood to persuade Alf Ramsey that he was worth considering for England. Ramsey had the idea that Peters couldn't head a ball, but he could, either defensively as a wing-half or as a goal-poacher, stealing up unnoticed on the blind side of opponents. He passes well too, anticipates shrewdly, works hard, thinks about it. Everything that's subtle, Peters does well.

The rest of the side is unaltered, but the pressures on all are growing. There is enormous public interest and a deep well of goodwill, but neither is bottomless. English crowds are not averse to booing their own side, never have been. The press have long been in the habit of investing England teams with the responsibility for delivering a national prestige far broader than a football field. Ramsey, because of his manner, because of what some pundits perceive as his preference for safety over style, remains on probation, despite the fact that England have lost only once in the last two seasons. We are in good health. Yet still doubts remain. We got nowhere against Uruguay. Ramsey needs goals and he needs them today.

There are other interested parties praying for an improvement. The BBC sports department won its argument for live evening airtime partly by making the case that the England team would advance to the later stages, taking most of the nation with them. If they falter now, the Corporation will be faced with the prospect of a gigantic flop and droves of disgruntled viewers demanding that normal service be resumed, as they say, as soon as possible. As *Grandstand* comes on air, counting down to a three o'clock kick-off, David Coleman takes his place overlooking Olympic Way hoping he'll have something to smile at the camera about by five. He hopes Ramsey will have something to smile about. Not that Ramsey ever actually smiles.

The Mexicans are in a changed strip of deep-red shirts and black shorts. Their supporters are making their now customary presence felt among the 92,000 crowd. But the English majority are louder, clapping, chanting, rattles loudly rotating. They are curious about the Mexicans and their fascination is increased by the behaviour of goalkeeper Ignacio Calderon just before the kick-off. As the England players limber up, Calderon sinks to his knees between his posts and offers up a prayer. The English have never seen anything like it. Does he only pray for himself or does everyone else on the pitch get prayed for as well?

As the captains exchange pennants and handshakes, the England reserves take up their places. Poor Connelly. Poor Ball. But, for all their disappointment, they can't help wanting England to win. The rest do too and in their impotence they give all the help they can. Norman Hunter is wearing exactly the same clothes as he wore for the Uruguay game and he's carrying exactly the same raincoat over his arm. And he's sitting next to Jimmy Armfield, to the left of him just the same. A lot of rubbish, superstition, but you can't be too careful. The press men pick their pens up, the cameras roll, the Mexicans chant, the English roar, the whistle blows and off they go. Calderon's way is not ours, but prayers of a kind are still said for England: for God's sake, score.

From the Mexican kick-off, Isidoro Diaz simply thumps the ball downfield and falls back. The entire Mexican team falls back. It quickly becomes apparent that it intends to stay back. There is an inexorable if saddening logic in this bald demonstration of intent, just as there was in their decision to attack against the French. They are the Group One outsiders, but they haven't crossed the Atlantic Ocean just to curl up and expire. They have three matches and they almost certainly need to win one of them. France looked the most penetrable opponents, so they attacked them. A draw wasn't ideal, but it has kept them in the running. Another draw today will do the same. They have a better chance of beating Uruguay next week than of beating England. Wembley, after all, is the home ground of the home nation. Any charity at the back will be an incitement to pillage. Such propositions are unacceptable. This is professional football.

Mexico, then, have already woven the dominant pattern of the game. England's job is to unravel it and displace it with their own more colourful design. But for those thousands looking on and willing England to fashion something fetching, a familiar feeling is growing. It is not peculiar to watching England. Anyone who has ever allowed their personal contentment to become dependent on the fortunes of a football team knows it only too well, especially if their team is expected to win, but failing.

At kick-off, hope springs eternal. The ninety minutes

to come are like a clean artist's canvas upon which all manner of bold brush strokes may soon be painted. For the first ten minutes, this sense of possibility can be disturbed only by some extreme event like an injury or the other lot scoring, but such occurrences are exceptions to the usual rule. Then your watch shows twenty-minutes gone and nothing much has happened. Nor has it looked like happening. The pieces aren't fitting together, the chemistry isn't there. Sympathy begins to give way to puzzlement, to impatience, then perhaps to irritation. Look at your watch again, and see that half an hour has gone and the game is about to start its slow, depressing slide towards a bleak, scoreless half-time . . .

The England fans start demanding: 'We want goals! We want goals!'

There's hardly been a sniff of one for all England's striving. They are aiming urgently at more fluidity, more complex forward movement than against their last opponents. The full-backs are pushing up, Stiles is going forward, Hunt and Greaves are haring about trying to extricate some space. But it's all so obviously anxious. Mexico stay dug in, only occasionally foraying over-ground. Diaz takes a long shot. Otherwise, it's just a slow dance, one step forward, three to the side. England's defence is almost redundant. And it may be an indictment of Ramsey that the player who comes closest to scoring is Bobby Moore. Cohen sends in a long, high, hopeful cross from the touchline not far inside the Mexican half. Moore, gambling, outleaps the defenders on the edge of the box and heads it just over

Calderon's crossbar. One for the scrapbook: a header at goal by Moore.

The forwards, though, look clueless. It's not for want of trying. Hunt is all over the place except in front of the goal with the ball at his feet. He's a popular player in the England squad, amenable, sturdy and fair. Send Hunt a poor ball and he'll make the effort to transform it into a good one. The Liverpool fans call him 'Sir Roger' because he is gallant, honest and brave. The England players say he's easy to find with a pass because you can spot his backside from anywhere. But it's all slog for Hunt so far and some of the southern fans have nominated him to be their whipping boy. Paine, meanwhile, is glued to the margin and is hardly in the game. Greaves is sparky, but sheds no light. Bobby Charlton scuds speculatively across the front line of Mexico's perpetually retreating midfield, pushing it wide, poking it vainly through, just beginning to flounder.

But then, from the centre-circle, his brother Jack spreads a ball to Stiles, waiting out wide on the Mexican frontier. Stiles traps it and, as is his habit, just lays it off to Bobby Charlton, then tears off into the box. Cohen sprints up on the outside but Charlton sets himself for a cross. It looks too wide, too shallow and towards no one in particular. But maybe Charlton has spotted Peters arriving silently and fashionably late. Either way, Peters, number 16, is there. He wins the header, propelling the ball back across the Mexican goal. Hunt is up like a jack-in-a-box and heads it high past Calderon.

There's a great shout and the players' arms shoot skywards. But the referee is shaking his head. Peters has been penalized, though no one can work out why. The Mexicans take a free kick as the groans around the stadium subside. Thirty-five minutes gone. In the stand sit Gordon Banks's German wife Ursula and their little boy, Bobby. There's a Mexican supporter next to them. He leans over and says to Bobby, Don't you worry, England will win this game and they will win the World Cup too. Down on the bench Ramsey sits, mostly silent, underlining the words of writers who've dubbed him Stoneface, Buddha, Sitting Bull. Among the reserves, spirits are beginning to sink. They all know as well as anyone that it's all going wrong. Even the ref is out to get them. They can hear the complaints of spectators, and they are an awful, ominous sound. There's nearly 90,000 of them. They've paid their money and they're moaning.

The Mexicans come upfield, tentatively. Wilson, Moore and Peters hold their ground. There's a pass inside, and Peters, intercepting, stabs a toe-end pass out to Hunt. There's a break on. Hunt side-foots it to Bobby Charlton and begins a long chase into the Mexican defence. The Mexicans, implausibly, are caught on their heels. A space has opened up and Charlton strides into it, carrying the ball at his feet. All through this tournament so far his play has been like his face sometimes seems, preoccupied and worried. But when he runs like this, he could still be a schoolboy in Ashington.

The Mexicans before him start to fall back, but more than usual have been caught upfield. Charlton keeps running, his stray hair trailing. The Mexicans keep backing off, some of them worried about Hunt. Greaves is hovering too, to the left. Charlton checks for a second, looks up, feints and swerves to his right, beautifully balanced. Both the England strikers are marked, but no one is within tackling distance of Charlton. He's twenty-two, twenty-three yards out, still running, but slowing, and it's as if for a slice of a second everyone else has stopped to hold their breath. Charlton shoots, right-footed, and launches the ball, low but rising towards Calderon's right-hand post. There's just long enough for everyone watching to take in that he's hit it, and it's flying, before it smacks into the stanchion supporting the rear of the Wembley net and England have scored.

Calderon has flown valiantly, but a wing and a prayer won't do. He's a century too late, and Charlton is yelling. It's what he always yells when a goal goes in: 'She's there!' He wheels away towards the crowd, runs, jumps and throws his raised arm forward in a salute that will be copied all over the country for months and years to come. Then he's down on his haunches and up again, to be embraced by Paine, then Hunt, then, as they turn instinctively back towards the centre spot, by Greaves with his jaunty walk. All around the stadium, from seat to bench to television gantry to the England players on the pitch, there is a massive feeling of relief. Charlton has brought the England campaign to life at last.

In the second half, though, they are unable to summon the style to plunder the troubled Mexicans.

Stuck in a rut and lacking in class, the Central Americans can't make a contest of it, but they can still hang about and frustrate. The high ball, often bombed in from a distance, is England's main recourse, but unless Big Jack has trundled forward there's no one who can make it pay off. Set pieces are more promising. Peters, who looks England's most composed player going forward, glances a header that's cleared off the line. Bobby Charlton has another shot, but this one is saved. There is no more inspiration until the seventy-sixth minute when Greaves makes his mark on the afternoon.

Surrounded for so long, he goes far into his own half to receive the ball from his own defence, distributes it neatly to Bobby Charlton near the left touchline and scampers on ahead. Charlton to Peters, back to Charlton, who strides on. Greaves is before him in a sliver of space, bawling for the ball as the crowd howl for a second, and Charlton shunts it to him at the perfect pace. Greaves controls it, and tries to place a shot past Calderon, who throws himself at the ball but can't hold it. He flounders as Hunt despatches the rebound. Sir Roger has had an indifferent game, but he's on the score-sheet yet again and England are top of Group One.

It has not been a vintage performance but it feels like heaven on earth. A crowd that would have been barracking anything less than twice that winning margin had England lowered themselves to play so feeble a nation as Mexico in a friendly, is instead brimming with patriotic pride. It now looks as though

England will make the quarter-finals, unless they come ruinously unstuck against France.

The day's other group games, though, give warning of sterner and crueller challenges to come. The big fixture is in Group Two with Argentina meeting West Germany at a drizzly Villa Park.

There is little to admire but plenty to fear. It begins in the first half when Jorge Albrecht, an Argentinian defender, executes a perfect rugby tackle on the impressive Helmut Haller. Astonishment greets this transgression, which is followed by a lengthy debate between Rattin and Konstantin Zecevic, the Yugoslavian referee five yards outside the Argentinian penalty area. Much expostulation. Much gesticulation. Many minutes pass. Meanwhile, Albrecht slips away, the Argentinians compose themselves and construct a defensive wall which requires considerable persuasion to move back the statutory ten yards. The free kick comes to nothing. There is one unsettling moment only when Perfumo, under pressure chasing back, heads the ball on to his own crossbar.

Mainly, it is low-level clog warfare. Beckenbauer, the young maestro against the Swiss, is cautioned for dangerous play. Rattin then applies the hatchet to him. Lorenzo, Argentina's manager, intervenes routinely from the touchline, joining any remonstrations going. But it is Albrecht who finally goes one assault too far. Fouled himself by another German player, he runs on to relieve his feelings on Weber, whom he hacks to the ground with the ball on its way to somewhere else. The referee is instantly engulfed by Argentinian players. Five minutes later, Albrecht walks to the dressing room to face almost certain suspension from the final group game. Argentina adapt and survive, passing the ball shrewdly to make up for the loss of a man. Artime, the Handsome One, is having one of his less delectable days, while Onega flowers only in flashes. But although the West Germans make great, muscular efforts they still get little change out of Rattin and his deputies. They stay top of the group, but they have yet to play the enigmas of Spain.

In Sunderland, Roker Park hosts Italy versus the USSR, the culture clash of the giants of Group Four. It is a crashing bore. The Italians seem subdued and inhibited for most of the match, fretting about the two big forwards who dwarfed the North Koreans and flapping when faced with the ingenuity of the winger Igor Chislenko. The Soviets have Yashin back, a magnificent red-gloved figure in black, dominating his area. What a shame for the 32,000 that he has next to nothing to do. In fact neither side manages to shoot straight for almost the entire afternoon.

It is Chislenko who scores the only goal after fifty-seven laborious minutes. After a dip and a jink he finishes with a left-foot shot high into the Italian net. Only in the last few minutes do the Italians rouse themselves, and an incredible goalmouth ruck is resolved when Yashin emerges from a pile of assorted players unruffled, holding the ball. The Soviets are now certain of being in the last eight. With four points from two matches, four goals scored and none conceded, they can now be overhauled by only one team in their group, ironically they've defeated today. As for the aristocrats of Italy, even in their subdued state they shouldn't have too much trouble at Ayresome Park against the minnows of North Korea and so secure their own quarter-final place.

Old Trafford enjoys the only scene of sustained artistry. Portugal soar to the top of the glorious Group Three by walloping Bulgaria three–nil. Eusebio wears a dressing from his scrape against Hungary, but the Bulgarians soon discover that he still has his eye in. Carvalho, the keeper who boobed against Hungary, is replaced by José Pereira of Benfica. There are two other changes, but the thrust of the forwards is the same. And fortune favours the brave once again. Torres sends over a cross in the eighth minute and Ivan Vutzoz obligingly heads it into his own net. Then comes Eusebio's first goal of the tournament. Simoes, the nimble Benfica winger, creates it for him. Eusebio's shot is sudden, fierce and too much for Naidenov to hold.

It is hard on the Bulgarians. At their best they would shine in any other group. The big Asparuhov shows again that the Portuguese defence can look rickety when tested. But their opponents demonstrate that there is more to their team than their incendiary number 13. The rest of the best of Benfica grace their offensive efforts. Jaime Graca, the serene Coluna, Simoes and Torres, who pounces on a sloppy back-pass to score his country's third. Two wins and a goal average of six. Portugal have put the big squeeze on Brazil, whom they meet at Goodison next.

As the Portuguese players leave Old Trafford they are mobbed by their own supporters and by a troupe of English fans. Most of them are men and boys waving autograph books. But, hey, some of them are girls! One asks one of the players to give her a big kiss. He is embarrassed! He runs away! But he may have to get used to this kind of treatment. After five days of competition, Portugal are the World Cup's rising stars.

Eight

Tuesday, 19 July 1966

ANOTHER THING about the North Koreans – no sex. Not for two years, apparently, while they've been drilled and groomed under military conditions in a secret mountain location. That's what the papers are saying, anyway. They've been made love to in Middlesbrough though. Without the North Koreans the town's unexpected part in the English World Cup drama would have been a comprehensive flop. The gates have been small – too small, it seems likely now, to recoup the cost of the many improvements made to Ayresome Park, despite the money from the government and the efforts of Charlie Amer with his box of carpet tacks. The draw was so wretched for them. Chile and the Soviet Union were never going to pack them in like the living legends who've graced the grander grounds of Manchester United and Everton. Even the Italians, today's guests, have had the shine knocked off them by their two uninspiring performances up the coast at Roker Park.

But the little men from the East have cheered things up, and they are glowing from the praise and attention. They are grateful for the welcome. They are anxious to be civil, they are eager to explain. They offer profuse thanks to the people of Teesside for their support and their affection – why, it's been almost like playing at home. They are driven by pride in their fatherland, they explain, but Middlesbrough will always have a place in their hearts.

As for their play, no one disputes it has been busy and determined and sporting to a fault. They have learned the rules of football and abided strictly by them. The deviousness and skulduggery that have dominated so much of the World Cup so far seem completely absent from their game. Otherwise Group Four has been depressingly uneventful. There are a little less than 19,000 today to see the North Koreans in what everyone expects will be their farewell game.

Not that the Italians are exactly brimming with self-belief. Their defeat by the Soviets was dismal, suffered by a team inexplicably different to that which beat the Chileans clinically enough. The most startling omission was of Rivera, one of their biggest stars. They left Sunderland in what looked suspiciously like a state of disarray, with Edmondo Fabbri already under fire from the fanatical press back home. Still, Rivera is back today and victory should be theirs. Since the Soviets are unlikely to lose to Chile tomorrow, even a draw will probably see them through to the second phase, and who knows how their fortunes may change. Football, it is often said, is a funny game.

The Koreans, in their red shirts, take the pitch to warm applause. It's a last chance for the Middlesbrough faithful to look fondly on the curiosities of their adopted team: their white bootlaces, their identical haircuts, their impossibly skinny goalkeeper Li Chan Myung. Among the crowd stands the tiny delegation of travelling North Korea supporters, all wearing cream raincoats. As the cry of 'KO-RE-A!' goes up from their new fans in the industrial north of England, the players raise their arms in salute.

The Italians, in azure blue with black shorts to make them more distinguishable on black-and-white television, begin the game positively. Mazzola, one of the few to be picked for all three games, lurks unnervingly around the North Korean danger zone. Barison raids. In midfield, Rivera looks decently attuned, and Bulgarelli, perhaps Italy's most consistent and committed player in the two previous matches, is putting himself about with his customary zeal. Enrico Albertosi in the Italian goal, wearing a thick grey jersey to go with the colour of the day, hardly sees the ball for half an hour. Fabbri's latest defence, an untried combination, looks set for an untroubled evening.

Chances are created, some of them good. After a smooth passing movement Marino Perani finds himself ten yards out with only the elfin Li Chan Myung to beat. His feeble shot is cleared, but the Middlesbrough crowd falls a little quiet. Still no goals. And with ten minutes to go until half-time Bulgarelli slams into a foul tackle on Pak Seung Zin near the centre-circle. He ends up on his backside, face twisted with pain. The crowd is sceptical at first: writhing is an Italian habit. But Bulgarelli isn't putting it on. Clutching a knee, he is carried from the field on a brown canvas stretcher by a couple of officials, a bloke in a blue cap and overalls

111

and a stray policeman. Italy are down to ten men, a further disruption of their fragile equilibrium.

The North Koreans have been pushed back so far. But they have tried to attack and they've shown no signs of surrender. Now the Italians must reorganize and reassess. Mazzola urges his team mates forward: one quick goal while they're still fresh and they can concentrate on conservation when fatigue begins to grip later in the game. But if there is an Italian contingency plan it soon requires urgent revision. Im Seung Hwi passes to Pak Doo Ik, who's spun free on the edge of the box. Bigger men in blue turn to bear down on him, but Pak Doo Ik is quick. He smites the ball firmly on the bounce and it travels fast at an angle towards Albertosi's right-hand post, where there is a most convenient gap. It's a goal, an authentic striker's effort, and almost unbelievable. North Korea one, Italy nil. The aristocrats go in at half-time scratching their heads. The North Koreans go in exultant. The Middlesbrough crowd lights up its cigarettes and considers the prospect of a miracle occurring right before its eyes.

There is an incredible energy about the North Koreans as they begin the second half. Han Bong Zin, pursuing a loose ball down the wing, clatters into the corner flag, snapping it in two. But nothing motivates the Italians like the fear of humiliation. These are proud men, fêted at home and feared abroad. Yet the hope invested in them by the Italian public is equalled by the wrath of its disillusion when things start going wrong. Failed Italian teams are pelted with vegetables at airports on their dismal return home. Now Mazzola, Facchetti, Rivera and company are having visions of flying tomatoes. Horror spurs them on.

But it's desperate stuff, and the North Koreans are fit and game. They challenge for every high ball, always lose it, but always recover to clear. Defending in swarms, they deflect the frantic thrusts of Mazzola, Perani and Barison. Li Chan Myung appears impossibly vulnerable, not because he is incompetent but because he looks so frail in his skimpy black kit. He cannot dominate his area like Yashin. Mazurkieviez or Banks. The opposing players look too big for him. The *ball* looks too big for him. But he keeps goal like a gymnast.

'KO-RE-A! KO-RE-A!' Rivera fades. The chanting of the Italian supporters fades. Hope fades, then dies. At the final whistle, the home crowd rises as one to its feet, shouting and cavorting as if Middlesbrough had just put six past Real Madrid. Some of them run on to the pitch and throw themselves on their heroes, picking them up and hugging them. This has been the greatest upset in World Cup history, as sensational as the United States' conquest of England in 1950. And, unless Chile beat the Soviets, North Korea are off to Goodison Park for a quarter-final match against the winners of Group Three. But the Italians have only one point out of six. Tomorrow, they will put on their sharp suits, their lovely blue shirts with the big wide collars and no tie and head off for a good haranguing back home.

Argentina are unhappy. Everyone loves North Korea but nobody loves them. Their tactics have been criticized and, following the sour stalemate with West Germany, FIFA's disciplinary committee has stepped in. The most damaging consequence is that Albrecht is, as expected, suspended for today's game against Switzerland. The committee also heard that several Argentinian players had tried to prevent referee Zecevič sending Albrecht from the field and that Lorenzo, the coach, had joined in from the touchline. Albrecht and Lorenzo were warned that if they repeated this behaviour they would be punished again, but more severely. The entire Agentinian team were instructed 'to play in a more sporting manner in future games'.

Disgruntled but unbowed they field the same team with the exception of Oscar Calics, Albrecht's replacement: Roma in goal, Perfumo, Ferreiro, Calics, Marzolini, Gonzalez, Rattin, Solari, their razor-edged winger Mas, the ball-player Onega, and Artime, the Handsome One. They have three points from their first two games and this should be the easiest. They need only a point, so they're taking no risks. The Swiss, doomed for sure unless they win, play their best football of the tournament in the first half, assaulting the Argentinians with their flowing 4–2–4. But in the whole of the first forty-five minutes they manage just one dangerous shot at Antonio Roma's goal. Argentina's attacks are characterized by precise circumspection. Rattin hits two long shots which breeze just over the bar. There is no undue exertion and no extreme behaviour. Nobody is booked. No one is sent off.

The shape of what might be regarded as a classic Argentinian performance forms rapidly after the interval. The Swiss defence clears sloppily and here's Artime escaping to the right of the goal, then pivoting and scoring with a shot that cannons in off the far post. It's his third in the cup so far. Handsome. Switzerland strive still harder and Roma has to make an outstanding save from Swiss striker Robert Hosp. Ever quick to respond to danger, Argentina pack their defence. The Swiss swing everything forward and duly fall for the counter-punch. A long high pass through the middle is pursued by Onega, who reaches it just in time to lob it over the advancing goalkeeper's head. Two–nil. Argentina are in the last eight and everyone's on edge.

Group One labours towards its denouement. Uruguay and Mexico contrive to produce a goalless draw from a match of surprisingly abundant scoring chances, principally for the Mexicans, who play prettily throughout. In their goal Calderon's prayers have been followed by his demotion in favour of Antonio Carvajal, who sets a record of appearing in his fifth World Cup series. He has little to do. Uruguay, who need just a point to make the last eight, set out to secure it and make a poor job of looking impregnable. In the last fifteen minutes the English spectators set up a chant of 'ME-HI-CO! ME-HI-CO!' in honour of Group One's most diverting and indefatigable visiting supporters. Tonight they will pack their sombreros, Uruguay will make enquiries about hotels in Sheffield, and England will reflect with satisfaction that even a one–nil defeat by France tomorrow night will put them into the last eight too.

José Augusto's been in the kitchen again, cooking dried fish and hot potatoes. Like ping-pong and cards, it passes the time. Eusebio's been listening to Portuguese ballads and taking care of that wound over his eye. After two matches in Manchester, it's to Goodison to encounter the shell-shocked Brazilians. Everyone is trying to stay cool. Only a three-goal defeat can leave the pretenders below the champions in Group Three and thereby vulnerable to the Hungarians, who play Bulgaria tomorrow. Anything better, and they are definitely through. They should be OK. But Brazil are still Brazil.

Only a decisive victory can keep the kings on their thrones. To observers, their old heroes have not looked up to such a feat, and the manager agrees. In the press box before the kick-off, the Brazilian journalists spot the ageing Garrincha, Djalma Santos and Altair sitting in the stand and rush down to the dressing room to find out what's up. They return to announce that Feola has made nine changes to the side blitzed by Albert, Farkas and Bene. Only the defender Lima and the winger Jairzhino remain. Even Gylmar the goalkeeper has been removed, replaced by Manga – known, unkindly, as 'Frankenstein'. The biggest news of all, though, is the return of Pelé.

There are 62,000 people at Goodison Park for this engagement between the two spiciest teams in the tournament. How dazzling they look as they come out of the dressing rooms, black men and Latin men in lemon and tangerine, crossing themselves as they step over the touchline. The thrill of Brazil has not worn off and the Portuguese, as everyone knows, have been pulling up trees down the East Lancs road. It's an encounter, too, between Eusebio and Pelé, the two diamonds each known by one name. Black footballers are a rarity in the English game, especially on Merseyside. Football in England is still a white man's form of expression. These Brazilians, these Portuguese, they're different, brilliant and strange.

Eusebio shimmers first. There's a free kick a full thirty-five yards out. Brazil build a wall and Manga waits. Eusebio just runs straight up and with his right foot sends the ball flashing past the stationary Brazilians, imparting a terrible dip which has Manga throwing himself forward to quell the treachery of the half-volley. He spills it, there's a scramble and he finally dives gratefully to kill it. But this is just an aperitif. Portugal are hungry. Like the crowd they have come to feast. The forward trio combine irresistibly and in unexpected ways. Torres has quicker feet than the average skyscraper. Simoes is much more than a hugger of touchlines. Eusebio burns like a long fuse and everybody holds their breath waiting for him to explode.

It happens again after fourteen minutes, and this time there are casualties. Eusebio goes into the Brazilian box. He's past the last man like an express train brushing the branches of an overhanging tree. But he's wide of the goal and travelling so fast and the ball is a long way in front of him. He cannot reach it. But he does. His weaker left foot telescopes and curls the ball back and across the waiting Manga's eyeline. The keeper, almost in disbelief, flaps at the cross and looks on in horror as it pops up towards Simoes. A header. A goal. The crown is slipping.

At the other end, Pelé strives, still spreading panic. In possession, anywhere within range of goal, he and the ball seem inseparable. He cannot be dispossessed or knocked off it. So instead he is fouled and laid low. The Brazilian trainer is Americo, a tiny little black man in a T-shirt and tracksuit trousers with belt pouches full of ointments and sprays. He scampers on to help the great man off the floor yet again. Eventually, Pele is up, but Eusebio is at them again at the other end. This time he is fouled but walks away after shaking hands with the offenders. Coluna, the captain, takes the free kick, flying it high towards Torres. It's almost slow motion as the centre-forward nods on to Eusebio, who, in turn, heads Portugal's second goal.

The sight of Eusebio celebrating is almost as captivating as his play. Arms aloft to form a perfect parabola he just runs anywhere, beaming fit to burst his cheeks, until finally his team mates catch hold of him and mob him. He radiates energy and pleasure. But ten minutes later Pelé is a picture of pity again. The offender is Joao Morais, a gristly, brown-haired tackler. First he dives in, misses the ball and clatters his studs into a leg. Pelé, still upright, peels away and Morais, frantic, throws out his boot again, this time to trip. Pelé goes down.

Eusebio goes over to him, stoops and briefly caresses his head. Americo and the team doctor Hilton Gosling lift Pelé by the armpits on to their shoulders, shuttle him to the strip of grass between the touchline and the cinder track, wrap a red blanket round his shoulders and go to work, helped by a St John ambulanceman in a peaked cap. They wrap a white bandage round his right leg just below the knee and pull his sock up into place. After five minutes Pelé goes back on the pitch, limping painfully. The applause is sympathetic and prolonged, but it cannot heal the hobbling number 10. Two–nil down and, with their champion winged, Brazil must now score five.

The second half is like the last act of a tragedy. For Brazil, the final outcome is now inevitable, but they cannot concede that they are doomed. Pelé, almost hopping, tries to compensate for invalidity with courage, struggling to contribute to Brazil's spasmodic attacks. Perseverance pays off as Rildo pulls one back, but it's the last hurrah of the giants as their fans strike up their final shimmies of samba.

The enduring triumphal image of this match will be of Eusebio rampant. He's cutting swathes through the yellow shirts now, letting fly almost at will. His face is all innocence, yet his body is all pace and power, a long torso, wide shoulders, piston legs. He moves with stunning speed yet effortless grace. His right foot is a hammer. The shape he makes a fraction after firing off his rocket shots leaves an indelible imprint on the memory: head down, his standing leg positioned at the point of perfect balance, the other handsomely extended in a flashing follow-through. It would make a gorgeous sculpture. They could cover it with gold plate and stick it on the bonnet of a million-dollar motor car.

Five minutes from time he brings an outstanding save from Manga, but it only forestalls the inevitable. A corner results and Augusto takes it. Torres flicks on. The ball bounces once in front of Eusebio, homing in.

He lashes it with a force and accuracy that are fatal for Brazil. Three–one, and he's on his victory run once more. When the final whistle blows, he bolts straight to the dressing room, the ball, his trophy, clutched to his chest.

The Brazilians leave with nothing but regret. Their defence of the title has been a tired disappointment. Most of their great stars have looked plain old rather than vintage. The teams they've fielded have flickered but failed to ignite, leaving an impression of surface flash and a severe shortage of substance. The Goodison crowds have enjoyed their extraordinary supporters and their good sportsmanship, the latter demonstrated once again as the two teams swap shirts, handshakes and backslaps. They have sympathized, too, with Pele, who has been kicked to bits throughout but is still generous in defeat. Yet Liverpool's soccer connoisseurs have had their passions satisfied by others.

Brazil have just got it wrong. And they've been wronged. There is justice in their private displeasure with some of the European referees. Persistent, often premeditated, fouling has received almost no appropriate punishment. Today, George McCabe of England has cautioned no one, not even the reckless Morais, and as a result the whole spectacle has been devalued. There is always a morbid satisfaction to be taken from the fall of empires, but the Brazilian players have put on no imperial airs. For the most part they are just big straightforward lads who've escaped from nowhere. In England they've filled their empty hours loafing about outside the gates of the Lymm Hotel, chatting amiably to reporters or showing off to passing Manchester girls.

Now it's a train to Euston station, a jet out of Heathrow, and many long hours of in-transit gloom.

For Pelé, the upset may be still more acute than for the rest. Injury kept him out of the crunch games in 1962 and now he's been denied again. There are compensations: he's already a dollar millionaire, earns £2000 a week, owns a bunch of skyscrapers in Rio and has been granted an audience with the Pope. At the Maracana stadium, the home of Brazil's national team, there's a plaque on the wall to commemorate the day he beat all eleven members of the other team before scoring. Pelé is still the nearest thing to the complete player, and still the ultimate individualist in an era of systematic defence. Before arriving in England he'd told David Miller of *The Times* that for him there could be no greater experience than the World Cup in England. It is the home of the game, he affirmed. Win or lose, after playing there he felt there could be little left to achieve. He may not be feeling that way now.

The Liverpool crowd is filing away with plenty to talk about. They have a quarter-final to look forward to next and then a semi. If England go that far, they are expected at Goodison. Meanwhile, up in the press box, the media army sits elbow to elbow getting its stories to bed. Somehow, they've squashed in eight hundred hacks. Earlier in the week an English newspaper quoted a Swedish reporter on the experience:

This is the first report ever filed by a journalist in a mousehole. I am wedged firmly between two planks and two cigar-smoking Brazilians in yellow sombreros and my typewriter is resting on the head of a Bulgarian journalist who winces every time I touch the keyboard. Every time I turn my head I swallow a burning cigar.

But there were compensations: 'Liverpool is the football city of England. The people here really are the supporters and friends of football.'

Now the typewriters are telling of how Liverpool is the place where the heavyweight title of football has changed hands. Here's the man from the *Daily Sketch*: 'Last week I said that Eusebio was challenging Pele for the title of best footballer in the world. I consider that Eusebio took the title away from him last night.' On another seat, the man from *L'Equipe*: 'Brazil put all its reliance on Pelé, but Portugal had Eusebio.' Elsewhere, the *Daily Mirror*: 'Eusebio, the snake who scored two great goals and made the third.' And down in Fleet Street, London, the *Mirror* sports desk is compiling its headline: 'Eusebio the Great Gave a Super Show'.

Goodbye Pelé. He was born in the little town of Bauru. Until he was ten, he played barefoot in the streets with a ball made of woollen rags. At fifteen, he joined Santos, leaving his apprenticeship as a shoemaker. At sixteen, he was picked for Brazil. Nine years on he slips, for now, into the shadow of Eusebio, who also used to play on the streets, who also left home when he was still in his teens, and who now has to leave the Goodison Park dressing room with an English policeman on both sides of him to keep a crowd of adoring, cheering, clamouring admirers at bay.

Nine

Wednesday, 20 July 1966

FRANCE TODAY, and Paine is out. This is tough on Paine. It has emerged that he was concussed for much of the match against Mexico, so the unimpressiveness of his performance is hardly surprising. Ian Callaghan is in. This is tough on Connelly, who is desperate for another go, but now seems to be further out of contention. It's also tough on Ball, who is prepared to play any team all on his own with both legs tied together. But it's great for Callaghan, twenty-three, a small man with a neat style, a wide dribbler who can also scheme from deeper positions. Like Peters, he has only come into the England picture at the very last minute, making his début in Scandinavia against Finland. Maybe he's the missing link in Ramsey's fitful attack.

Paine's knock on the head may be the decisive reason for his demotion. After all, other unimpressive performances have not been punished in the same way. Stiles in particular put on a poor show against the Mexicans, confirming his and Ramsey's critics in their belief that England are severely short of creativity in midfield. But in the camp Stiles is a lucky mascot, the 'Toothless Tiger' as he has been dubbed by those who see him as a great English character rather than a moderate English footballer more preoccupied with damaging shins than carving openings. Stiles himself is meticulous in his efforts to make sure that luck attaches to him. It isn't only Norman Hunter who's been sticking to the same civilian clothes on match days as he wore the last time England didn't lose, far from it. But Stiles takes things that obsessional bit further. With him, it has to be the same shirt as for the last game that England didn't lose, and the same tie, same shoes, same socks, same underpants and even the same pair of cufflinks.

Whether or not Nobby's attention to the detail of his smalls and accessories has made the vital difference, the England camp feels a lot luckier now. Not only has the team won a match but last night's stalemate between Uruguay and Mexico has made the task much easier in that the French are now obliged to make an open game of it. Bobby Charlton has enjoyed rave reviews for his goal against Mexico. Peters has impressed and is quietly satisfied that he has stayed in the team. Hunt has scored a goal, which is what he's there for. The defence, of which Stiles is the first line, has done what it is there for too: it hasn't been scored against. None but the West Germans and the Soviets can still say the same. Despite the fact that England have not looked a great team, of the eleven picked today only one could be said to have decisively failed to fulfil his remit so far: Greaves, England's greatest goalscorer, who has yet to score a goal. It's not for want of trying, but he hasn't found his stride and what little good fortune has been going has fallen at the feet of Hunt.

Greaves has long envisaged himself at the heart of England's challenge for the cup. Deep down, he's not as sure of himself as his street patter suggests. Notching one today would be a comfort.

The French, meanwhile, need to raise their game in all departments. Once they had a reputation for football that flowed as beautifully as anyone's. Now they must try and regain it. They've been surprised by the Mexicans and overpowered by Uruguay. The curly, fair-haired Robert Herbin has been recalled after being dropped for the Uruguay game, and the clever Jacques Simon has been retained. A feat of stunning escapology is now required. They seem unlikely to provide it, but there may be some pleasure in watching them try.

England's victory on Saturday seems to have bumped up the attendance. There are more than 98,000 in Wembley today, the biggest gate so far for an England match, even though the stakes are lowest. In Sunday's *Observer* Hugh McIlvanney concluded a caustic review of the win over Mexico by expressing surprise that the crowd had been moved to sing with such enthusiasm. 'Either Wembley audiences have changed fundamentally or there should be dope tests for spectators.' But enthusiasm for the cause is clearly growing. It does seem the case that the World Cup has tapped some formerly unsuspected source of soccer patriotism in the capital. Football is becoming the biggest news around, bigger even than the £500 million-worth of government spending cuts announced today by Harold Wilson in his latest attempt to stall the sterling crisis precipitated by a thousand faceless speculators, the addition of fourpence a gallon on petrol duty and a restriction on the amount of money people can take out of the country to a mere fifty pounds.

No wonder the Wembley throng, clapping and chanting, is looking for more goals. But the first memorable incident of the match involves the referee and Nobby Stiles. Untypically, it is not the result of Stiles being party to an affray. In fact, England's emblem collides with Arturo Yamasaki of Peru and spends the next few minutes in a state of unfamiliar incapacitation. Soon after, the French have a more serious casualty. Herbin is reduced to a limping passenger and seems unlikely to recover. The air of farce thickens when the half-mobile Frenchman makes the most threatening goal effort of the first half-hour with a brave diving header that misses the target but has Banks on his toes. France move the ball subtly and purposefully at first, making the England back four go efficiently through its basic paces. Yet it is England who get it into the net. Callaghan crosses and the vaporous Peters solidifies to jump and head beyond Marcel Aubour. The ball falls to Greaves, who guides it in from point-blank range only to turn and discover that the linesman has flagged for offside.

The longer he is denied, the more Greaves busts his guts to get in on the act. Moore clears up a French attack and finds his friend and room mate waiting wide on the halfway line. Greaves controls the ball and sets straight off for goal. It's the archetypal Greaves scamper, hips swivelling, feet skipping, would-be tacklers caught napping on the turn. Bobby Charlton is free, Hunt is free, but Greaves knows where the goal is and that's where he's heading. He looks up only to take aim as he approaches the edge of the box, and as the crowd gets to its feet ready for the finale of this show of sorcery, he takes a potshot with his right foot. The ball trundles, half-hit, into Aubour's hands. Greaves, hands on knees, gasps for breath.

The truth is that it's another unsatisfactory game not just for number 8 but for the team as a whole. England look the stronger, but they don't really cohere. Then, with half-time nearing, Bobby Charlton cuts in from the right. This time the hammer is in his left foot. Aubour leaps to cover his top-right corner and touches the ball over as the crowd, which has been aching for another Charlton thunderbolt, goes 'oooh' and 'aaah' and fills the air with consoling applause. Greaves takes the corner kick short to Stiles, who half loses it, then digs straight in to win it. Nobby in a nutshell. He steers it back to Greaves, who spots Jack Charlton, still up for the corner. Greaves aims a first-time lob in his direction. The French have taken their eye off the big man, who always walks out last. Charlton, never elegant, nods the falling ball against the foot of the post from two feet out as the French dash back hopelessly late, wondering if they might once more be saved by the offside law. They wonder about it some more when Hunt, all alone, rolls the rebound into the net to put England in front. Some of them race to the touchline imploring the linesman to wonder about it too. To no avail. Cynics at home watching the action replay might remark meaningfully on the fact that today is Roger Hunt's birthday.

Jacques Simon leads the last-ditch French assault. He's been all over the pitch, prompting and battling. Now he's got Banks diving full length to save a header. It's just after half-time and the England goalkeeper didn't exactly have his hands full in the first forty-five minutes, but despite this tedium, despite being only just back from his break, Banks is ready and waiting. That's one reason why Alf Ramsey picks him every time.

At this rate Peters is going to be an automatic selection, too. He wins another header under Aubour's nose and Bobby Charlton nets with a volley, but again the referee denies England. Yet, as the evening sunshine fails, it becomes inevitable that England are going to go through. With fifteen minutes left the French, for whom Herbin is still hobbling, need to score three times with no reply against Banks, Cohen, Wilson, Stiles, Jack Charlton and Moore.

It's a tall order. And then they lose their inspiration, Simon. Stiles goes to tackle him, but Simon is too quick, and by the time the England man has made harsh contact with Simon's leg the ball is already heading somewhere else. There is no whistle, so no foul. With Simon prostrate, the ball finds Bobby Charlton out on the wing, the position he has played in for England so many times in the past. He crosses, a Frenchman makes contact, but the ball is not properly cleared. Simon is still in trouble and maybe the French have lost concentration. The loose ball comes to Callaghan, the World Cup débutant. He has time and space, and he centres perfectly towards his Liverpool team mate Hunt, who just picks up his heels to head his second, the ball slipping through Aubour's fumbling fingers on the line.

The French are incensed. They have a man down injured after what looked like a dreadful foul, yet the referee has just waved play on while the English clinch victory and guarantee France's exit. The match duly ends with the score at two–nil. England have finished at the top of Group One with five points from a possible six, scoring five goals and (still) conceding none. It's an impressive record on paper, but the statistics deceive. The English have never looked like losing, but even with home advantage they have not yet looked capable of beating the best in the field. And though most of the crowd go home satisfied, a few partisans give the England players a futile piece of their rather uninteresting minds. There's always one near you. This time he's close to the seats from where the England reserves have been watching, groaning and shouting and suffering as usual. The big mouth gets to Geoff Hurst, who turns and invites him, though not in so many words, to keep his opinions to himself. It all gets a bit overheated and Mrs Hurst, sitting close by, becomes involved saying, all right, Hursty, leave it, let it go. The jibes hurt because they contain a grain of justice. England still have a bit to prove.

The rest of the group programmes reach their conclusions too. Chile's prospects against the Soviet Union are enhanced from the start by the Soviet management's decision to make nine changes from the side that beat Italy in order to give their best players a rest. But they lose an early goal to the winger Valeriy Porkujan. As the first half goes on, Chile get stronger but convert only one of a number of chances, Ruben Marcos the scorer. In the second half their finishing gets worse still, even though they are cheered on by a Roker Park crowd desperate for anything to get excited about in this, the last of the three dismal group games placed before it. And four minutes from the end a long clearance from a ragged Soviet defence finds Porkujan, who scores his second to win the game. The result from Group Four is not sensational, but its implications are. By beating Chile the USSR confirm North Korea in second place in Group Four. The Chileans exit the World Cup as utterly downcast as the Italians on Tuesday. The North Koreans can anticipate their astonishing prize of a quarter-final against Portgual at Goodison Park.

At Old Trafford, the Hungarians play the already doomed Bulgarians before a crowd of 33,000, most of them hoping for a reprise of the virtuoso football from Albert and Bene that sent the Brazilians into a spin at Goodison Park. They get it, albeit belatedly and in a diluted form. It is Bulgaria who take the lead after Gelei in Hungary's goal races out of his area with the aim of beating Asparuhov to a through-ball. He fails, turns, launches a flying tackle in a frantic effort to save his bacon and fails with that as well. Asparuhov scores into an empty net. For the next twenty-five minutes the

Hungarians seek and gradually find some of their former fluidity, but their opponents' defence is resolute: until, that is, Ivan Davidov puts the ball in his own net. Then, with a minute till the interval, captain Meszoly gives Hungary the lead, creating the climate in which his team can flower in the second half. Bene scores their third with an impressive header after fifty-four minutes. Hungary finish second to Portugal in the powerful Group Three. They meet the USSR next.

The best football of the day is played at Villa Park, where Spain have to defeat a West German team needing a draw to secure qualification from Group Two. Dismissing any notion that discretion might be the better part of valour, the Spanish make five changes which include the replacement of the enervated Suarez and the distended Gento. From the kick-off they go forth boldly against the West German defence and prove it to be permeable when José Fuste leaves Tilkowski to pick the ball out of his net for the first time in the tournament.

The West Germans have also made a couple of changes. Haller, so smooth in the first two games, is rested this time and manager Schoen brings in Lothar Emmerich of Borussia Dortmund. Although Emmerich was the Bundesliga's leading goalscorer last season he is seen as a bit of a mystery. For the most part he plays wide on the left and gets his goals with lethal left-foot shooting. Otherwise, he seems ordinary and too

131

unsophisticated to disconcert a Spanish defence blessed with the excellent José Iribar in goal.

Yet as the rattled West Germans strain to get on terms, Iribar finds himself diving to save at the feet of Held and menaced by the head and the feet of the incorrigibly robust Seeler. The Spanish have demonstrated nerve and verve, but the West Germans equal it with steel and skill. And close to half-time they show that they have a manager of winning judgement. A throw-in by Held finds Emmerich running towards the Spanish by-line. He crashes the ball past Iribar from an implausibly tight angle to put the West Germans level. Given the two teams' respective needs, there seems every likelihood that the second half will see the Spanish pressing and the West Germans holding fast to the single point they require. Yet the players contrive a display of fine attacking football, with both sides coming close to a second goal before Seeler scores clinically six minutes from the end following a cross by Held. It is a goal which places West Germany at the top of Group Two with a quarter-final against Uruguay to come and which leaves Argentina, runners-up on goal average, to face England at Wembley.

Even in the most tranquil circumstances England versus Argentina would look like a tie of high and particular tensions. Given the events during the last nine days it fills even the most disinterested with trepidation. From the defiant pragmatism of the Uruguayans in their opening match against England to the Argentinians' conflagrations with the West Germans and throughout the brutalizing of Pele in his two games at Goodison Park, pre-tournament mistrustfulness between South American and European football has steadily grown to the point where it is ready to burst into the open. The dominant proportion of English and other European referees, the manipulation of the draw and the attitude of the various English crowds to which they have been exposed have combined to heighten South American suspicions that FIFA and the FA have somehow colluded – if not actually plotted – to make it almost impossible for a team from their part of the globe to win the World Cup in England.

They bridle at the English stereotype of Uruguay and Argentina as oily assassins, all short temper and sharp practice. They also regard the approach of some English players as shameless thuggery dignified as unvarnished valour. And they are not wholly alone in their distastes. Nobby Stiles's tackle on Jacques Simon has ensured that as well as celebrations there are ructions in English football circles. Tonight's BBC panel of experts is Jimmy Hill, the genial Joe Mercer, a former England international, now manager of Manchester City, and the Northern Irishman Danny Blanchflower, who captained the Tottenham team that won the League and FA Cup double in 1961 and advocates open, attractive football with unusual eloquence. The Stiles incident divides them. Hill is the professionals' champion and 'PR' are his middle initials. He says Nobby meant no harm. But Mercer is not so sure. And Blanchflower says the incident has ruined the game for him. By the end of the evening there are murmurs in the air that Stiles will have to go.

The debate is not confined to pundits. After the game Ramsey asks Stiles privately for his explanation for the tackle. Stiles insists that although it was a poor one it was not malicious. Ramsey listens, then tells Stiles to put the whole thing out of his mind: if there's worrying to be done, he'll be the one to do it. But Ramsey has other worries too. England's play today has not pleased him. He's sensed complacency and he isn't having that. In the dressing room, he upbraids his team. Wilson, for no very apparent reason, comes in for particular disapproval. Of the outfield players, only Hunt is praised. Then there's the problem of an injury to Greaves. He's finished the game with a gashed shin that requires medical treatment. Six stitches are inserted in a wound that will keep him out of the next game and probably any semi-final that may follow.

And of course the context for Ramsey's anxieties is a cause for anxiety itself. Uruguay, Mexico and France collectively provided an unexceptional test which England passed without much merit. Argentina, by contrast, look like a very good team indeed. Moreover, they are a team with a point to make not only on their own behalf, but on behalf of their nation and, indeed, the football culture of their continent. To humble England in front of a Wembley crowd would be almost as great a prize as winning the World Cup itself.

Ten

Saturday, 23 July 1966

STILES STAYS. Ramsey told him yesterday after a training session at Highbury. Sensing the midfielder's anxiety, he took the necessary step to dispel it: 'Incidentally, you might like to know you will be playing tomorrow.' Alf and his understatements. Stiles has been wretched with worry as the furore over his tackle on Simon has raged. Quite apart from the critics on television and in the newspapers, FIFA has also intervened. Although the referee restricted himself to a word of warning at the time, a watching FIFA official made use of his rather bizarre power to 'book' a player from the stand. The matter then came before the disciplinary committee, which confirmed the caution, citing 'rough play', and then requested Denis Follows as head of the English Team Delegation to warn Stiles that 'if he were reported again, serious action would be taken'.

All this was duly conveyed to Ramsey, its formal wording also conveying a deeper diplomatic unease: England is the host nation and we can't have our own side sinking to the levels we've deplored in Johnny Foreigner from down South Atlantic way; a cocktail of Stiles and Argentina would be a close cousin of Molotov's;

perhaps number 4 ought to sit this one out. Such a suggestion does not appear to have been made explicit. But, however nebulous, it was always likely to have the opposite effect to that apparently intended. Ramsey's disdain for his employers' top brass has long bordered on outright rudeness and he has continued to guard jealously the autonomy he insisted on as the key term of accepting his job. He picks the team, no one else.

Stiles, meanwhile, is affronted as well as distressed. Wounded innocence comes to him readily when he is accused of being little more than a licensed destroyer. The way he tells it he's tough-but-honest, he's hard-but-fair, he's been given a reputation he does not deserve and now every goody-two-boots in town is trying to make it stick. He's had a commiserating telegram from Billy Bremner, a little Scot who does a similar job for Leeds. It reads: 'Don't let them get you down.' The moaners and the buffers in blazers have got it in for him, thinks Nobby, but the professionals understand. Luckily, Ramsey is one of them.

Another happy man is Stiles's Hendon Hall room mate: Ball has been brought back. It's bad luck on Callaghan, who had a fair game against the French. It compounds the dismay of Connelly. But Ball had half an inkling he'd return against Argentina. He'd antici-pated that Ramsey would think that this was Ball's kind of game. Ball is perseverance personified, prepared to forage ceaselessly in the thickest undergrowth, and against the massed snapdragons of Argentina that has to be an asset. He's a self-conscious northern toughie, too: if they want a fight, they can have one.

The confirmation of Stiles, the rehabilitation of Ball and the inclusion of Hurst demonstrate the fundamentals of Alf Ramsey's England to a greater degree than is immediately apparent. At first sight his preference for the first two simply confirms the contention of some that the manager's basic instincts are negative. Yet this ignores not only the three preceding matches but also the three preceding years, in which he has routinely picked at least one winger and often two. It also ignores his enduring faith in Greaves as the provider of something special, something extra. Rather, the placing of numbers 4 and 7 in the front line against such fearsome foes given all the present circumstances demonstrates Ramsey's intense determination to be flexible, to be pragmatic and to risk unpopularity in the consuming interests of effectiveness. With Peters retained, he also demonstrates a willingness to experiment. His use of 4–3–3 against Spain in December had seemed daring at the time. Now he seems to be deploying another formation, virtually 4–4–2, with only Hurst and Hunt as specialized frontmen.

However, the full extent of his single-mindedness, his immersion in the professional ethos, and his deafness to outsiders remains concealed by common knowledge of Greaves's six stitches. Because the injury is no secret, Hurst's recall to the England team for his first World Cup match is accepted as inevitable. What only Ramsey, probably Shepherdson and possibly Cocker know is that Greaves was likely to have been discarded anyhow. The great man's muse is eluding him and he hasn't even been on hand for a tap-in. The suspicion remains that

his illness has weakened him. Then there's his past failure in Chile. With Hunt, by contrast, you know what
you're going to get. Whatever he's asked for he'll provide it for ninety minutes, however thankless. And to
those who complain that Hunt will never provide the
kind of magic moment which managers have no right
to expect, only thank their lucky stars for, then a riposte
lies in recent statistics. Hunt, eight goals in ten England
games this season; Greaves, five in nine, four of them
in one game against feeble opposition, and none in the
last five.

Given this, the case for Hurst over Greaves is persua-
sive. Like Hunt he is a grafter, but he's also a six-footer
whose great strength in the air may open up the aerial
avenue to goal in a way that Greaves never could. But
Hurst also brings with him some of the finesse of the
West Ham 'academy' already demonstrated in the
World Cup by Martin Peters and Bobby Moore. Ron
Greenwood is scrupulous about instilling what he calls
'good habits' in his players. He's a great one for considered passing, intelligent positioning and cultivated
ploys made automatic through dedicated practice.

Apart from his England trio he has lots of skill and
polish at his club: Budgie Byrne, Ronnie Boyce, John
Sissons. Greenwood has taught them all a move he first
picked up and adapted from the 1953 Hungarians. On
the West Ham training ground at Chadwell Heath he
puts them through an exercise using wooden posts set
in concrete-filled buckets to represent defenders. One of
these is placed near a touchline about thirty yards out.
The players are instructed to deliver crosses towards

the near goal post, first bending the ball around the dummy defender. As the ball loops in, other players run from deep positions to intercept its flight and flick it towards the goal. The beauty of the move is that it invests an early cross with greater menace, catches opponents by surprise and pulls defenders out of position, all at the same time. It's mostly just a matter of co-ordination and timing. 'Simplicity is genius,' Greenwood likes to say.

At Wembley, the sun is shining for the first time since the Queen said her piece at the opening ceremony. Down Olympic Way, the crowds seem thicker and their chatter more excited than for England's group games. The whole mood is more intense. There are more men calling out, urging punters to invest in scarves, metal badges and rosettes. There are still plenty of collars and ties, but many have indulged in the permissible informality of an open-necked shirt. Those in fancy dress and silly hats are still a small minority but, even so, it's a minority that has grown. This is as near to carnival mood as an English football crowd has ever been.

The change requires little explanation. After the sparse excitements of the first phase, they are about to experience the enhanced drama of the knock-out stages. From now on there can be no strategic playing for a draw in anticipation of easier fixtures to come and no result will be assessed in terms of its effect on group positions and goal averages. At the end of this afternoon, England will either be in the semi-finals of the World Cup or out of it altogether. It may take extra time. It may even go to the flip of a coin. But there will be no hiding-place, no second chance. And, just to spike the occasion with menace, the other team is both accomplished and ruthless. As it takes its seats inside the stadium, the crowd is nervous like wild-west townsfolk at five minutes to noon awaiting a shoot-out in the street. The analogy is strengthened by some of Argentina's fans: they are wearing tin helmets and carrying replica machine-guns. Olé.

In the North dressing room, Ramsey addresses his men. He is renowned for his habit of putting players just that little bit on edge, and more than one can recount occasions when his tongue has cut them down for exhibiting the most trivial symptom of complacency. This typically happens when a squad breaks up after a match is over. See you next time, then, Alf. Oh, you think I'll be picking you then? Uh, OK, well, er, hope to be seeing you again then, Alf. But when he wants them filled with confidence, when he wants to concentrate their loyalty to each other and to him, he softens this brittle, managerial distance. He allows an ambience much closer to intimacy, and his manner becomes almost cryptic. The players become 'gentlemen'. Fellow gentlemen, perhaps. Gentlemen, I think we know what kind of job we have on our hands today . . . They do. Above all it has been impressed on them that they must remain patient and calm. The Argentinians are talented, shrewd, unscrupulous and in a bitter mood.

Stiles is given a special job. He has to keep a close eye on Onega, at his best a throwback to the famous days of South American ball skills and the instigator of

Argentina's most creative moves. The back four, meanwhile, are urged to keep their nerve. There may be long periods of boredom, but these will be punctuated at unpredictable moments with swift surprise attacks. The art of Artime the Handsome One needs no introduction. But the golden rule is not be frustrated into rash tackles or dashes out of position. The Argentinians are so adept at punishing impetuosity, they actively cultivate it.

In the tunnel, the England players see their opponents in the flesh, some for the first time since Rio two years ago, some for the first time ever. For television's sake England, in accordance with the etiquette of home teams, have changed their shorts from black to white, but their shirts are the same. The Argentinians' kit seems better suited to the weather. Their regency stripes come in short sleeves today, suitable for southern-hemisphere-like conditions. England aren't so used to those. The captain Rattin gathers his men around him for a pep talk. He looks imperious, instructing in Spanish. He gestures at the England players as if to say, 'These English, they are nothing.'

The teams are led out by Rudolf Kreitlein of West Germany, a short, pointy-faced figure with a military walk and a shiny pate which gleams amid his remaining hair like a bird's egg in a nest. At the centre-spot he presides over Moore and Rattin's ritual exchange of tokens and hollow well-wishes. The Argentinian offers the hint of a regal bow. The Wembley crowd has come to see pale blue as the hue of villainy. As the teams line-up for the kick-off there's an edge in the atmosphere.

The cries of 'ENG-LAND!' and the Brazilian clapping chant have a special urgency.

The pattern of the match is set within a handful of minutes. The English foul the Argentinians, the Argentinians foul the English. Peters is body-checked, Jack Charlton is trampled as he falls after a corner. Herr Kreitlein blows his whistle frequently and wags his finger a great deal. Argentina defend in depth, their midfield players moving the ball warily among themselves. Rattin is at the hub, strolling, gesturing, directing his fellows around the field. They prowl and dart, but only rarely attack. Stiles stalks Onega. Bobby Charlton grazes a post from a corner-kick and Hurst shoots wide from twenty-five yards. It is eighteen minutes before Banks has to exert himself, saving a shot from Mas. Mostly the Argentinians just eye the opposing goal from the fringes of the final third, goading the English defenders, willing one of them to lose patience, break rank, commit soccer suicide. Nobody does, but there's a long, long way to go. The English defenders talk to each other or, rather, they shout instructions and encouragement above the urgings of the crowd. Cohen, the elder Charlton, Moore and Wilson bark at each other to hold formation, to watch out behind you, man on, don't go, don't go. Stiles shouts at everyone. It's edgy, untidy, and it looks like staying that way.

The Argentinians are talking too. They talk to each other just like the English, but they also talk to Herr Kreitlein. Rattin especially talks to him almost constantly, stooping to bend the little German's ear, a study in relentless remonstration. Kreitlein swats him away agitatedly, directs play to continue, whistles for some further foul and the whole weary pantomime starts all over again. Then Rattin fouls Bobby Charlton, not a savage foul but a sly one, which has the English crowd howling at this long, dark, smouldering man, now reduced in their eyes to this greasy Argentine dago. And again Rattin's bending over the little official, hands waving, tongue wagging. Herr Kreitlein brings out his little black notebook and his pen. He jots Rattin's name and his number, a narrow black 10. Then Artime, the Handsome One, gets booked. Rattin goes to Herr Kreitlein to plead his striker's case, stooping again, bending his ear again, remonstrating again as the afternoon sun beats down. So Herr Kreitlein reaches up and taps him on the shoulder and, with a parade ground flourish, points towards the touchline.

There's a great roar from the English fans, followed by a moment of suspended belief as the stadium comes to terms with the fact that Rattin has been sent off. Then a whole posse of players in blue-and-white stripes descends on Herr Kreitlein as Rattin, shoulders sloping, hands held low on hips, looks away and strikes a pose of cruelly injured disbelief. It's a passion play, it's a latin inferno, it's chaos. It's an alien spectacle, something that couldn't happen here. What the English don't understand is that the Argentinians are certain that they are being fixed, conspired against, conned, before their very eyes. Six Argentinians are all around Herr Kreitlein. Roma rushes up from his goal, shouting and screaming. Seeking a few yards of space on the verdant Wembley turf, Herr Kreitlein shuttles backwards at high speed, clicks his heels, looks at Rattin and repeats his stiff-arm instruction.

Rattin gathers himself and strides massively, head now returned to its customary fine elevation, towards the touchline where Argentina's benchmen in their blue tracksuits are going completely insane. The captain's body language insists that this cannot be happening, something must be done. They all fall into a voluble huddle, arms waving distractedly, apparently bent on doing anything but walking resignedly away. Soon other players have joined in and Herr Kreitlein, whistle wedged between pursed lips, cannot restart the game. He too marches to the touchline, flapping at the huddle to make it desist, disperse, go away. Rattin bending low again, plucks pugnaciously at his captain's armband as if in a last, despairing, shrugging attempt to persuade the referee that this is all some crazy injustice, that it is a captain's prerogative to argue with the referee. Harry Cavan, the FIFA commissaire, joins the pitchside congregation. So too does Ken Aston, the match officials' liaison officer. So too does one, then two, then three, then four Metropolitan policemen, all but the first of them wearing peaked caps with sparkly trim.

In the crowd, down at the front, men in sunglasses and shirtsleeves, some of them wearing knotted handkerchiefs on their heads, gesticulate and shout. Get off, you dago! Send 'em all off, ref! Off! Off! Off! Incredible scenes. *Incredible!* In the seats behind the England bench, Armfield, Hunter, Connelly and all look on in amazement. Like their comrades on the pitch they'd been under no illusions about what the Argentinians could be like. But events are now taking a turn which amazes even hardened campaigners like them. On the pitch Banks, Moore and Jack Charlton stand and wait. Wilson sits on the ball and looks up at the scoreboard. England nil, Argentina nil. But also, just to add to the pandemonium and provoke another resounding cheer . . . Portugal nil, North Korea three . . . *Portugal nil, North Korea three!*

But no, none of this is a dream. One of the policemen in a cap with sparkly trim points Rattin and a blue tracksuit emphatically towards the tunnel way beyond Roma's goal and slowly the Argentinian captain begins the long trek some sixty regulation yards along the wrong side of the touchline as the crowd gawps and barracks and, in a couple of unrestrained cases, wave two fingers in a most unChurchillian salute. The match restarts, and Herr Kreitlein, who may have just changed the course of soccer history, goes about his busy business. But many eyes are still on the disgraced captain, crestfallen in all but posture. On the England bench and among the reserves they are struck by the look of the man as he passes, a vast vision of brooding fury. He walks on, eyeballing his tormentors in the wooden seats behind the barrier, past billowing Union Jacks, stopping briefly to stare wistfully back at the unfolding, stop-go action from which he has been expelled, then on past a couple of English boy scouts sitting by a corner flag graced with Arthur Bew's patriotic design. Rattin plucks at it absently, contemptuously, before finally pushing through the crowd of curious military bandsmen in maroon berets gathered in readiness to parade at half-time, past the regimental goat in its finery, and into the deep, warm nothingness of an early bath. The crowd, its lust satisfied for the present, cries: 'ENG-LAND! ENG-LAND!'

As his players suck their half-time oranges Ramsey's urgent message is to remain calm. No English names have been taken, but England have committed the greater number of fouls. And the Argentinians, even without their captain and even though facing the sweltering, nationalistic malice of the Wembley cauldron, are still messing up England's rhythm, and still holding their own. There is nothing for it but to maintain patience and await the opening that surely must come on a baking summer's day against ten men. The England team walks back on to the pitch to a great chorus of cheers, the Argentinians to a hail of litter, fruit and catcalls.

Herr Kreitlein peeps his whistle and the pattern is as before. Argentina foul, England foul. From a corner Jack Charlton tangles with Roma, and someone kicks him on his way down. His brother Bobby rushes over to harangue the referee, a sight that is rarely, if ever, seen. The fracas prompts a FIFA official in the stand to 'book' both the Charlton brothers, just as Stiles had been against France. Argentina hold the ball, England chase it. When they get it, they labour. Although Ball forays forward to support them, Hunt and Hurst find little joy. The configurations of both teams mean the two English frontmen are playing almost exclusively with their backs to the Argentinian goal, man-marked and misused. Lesser spirits would be tempted to hide away. Every time they break for space they are likely to be tugged back or tripped. Hurst is clattered and battered. Hunt, trudging away after the collapse of yet another England attack, feels a mighty whack on the back of his leg, turns around and sees Marzolini walking speedily away. With the constant threat of what feels like GBH it is hard to pay attention to their proper jobs of running and chasing and pulling the thick, retreating lines of Argentinian defence out of shape.

It's all becoming a desperate sweat. The Argentinians are skilled and composed. Their football is the more polished. Mas almost puts them ahead. England look clueless, lost, and it is a rare moment when Bobby Charlton breaks forward or Peters glides into advanced space. He manages it, though, after seventy-seven minutes, and Wilson, a measured distributor, slides the ball forward to him. Peters, down near the touchline, looks up and sees a defender coming across to cut him off. He shapes elegantly and loops a long cross around him, and on towards the momentarily vacant nearer corner of the Argentinian goal area. Perfumo is not there to meet it. Roma stays put. Hurst arrives. It's a high centre, almost too high, but Hurst, still moving at speed, translates forward movement into upward thrust, twists his body in mid-air, connects with his forehead and glances the ball downwards and backwards, sending it bouncing past the left hand of the startled Roma and into the goal, leaving everyone else on their heels and Hurst peeling away and bounding towards the line of photographers. It's a West Ham goal, a Ron Greenwood goal, a goal that arrives from nowhere by way of Chadwell Heath.

Peters executes a spontaneous forward roll. Hurst, arms aloft, turns to his team mates, his smile sweet with relief. Ball leaps into his arms like an excited child. As the pair trot back towards the centre circle, they are joined by Banks in his yellow jersey, who has run a hundred yards from his own goal-line to praise the scorer. A few England supporters spill on to the pitch, delighted and vindictive.

The last thirteen minutes frizzle irritably away, and the joy of the England players at the end of the game resembles that of escaped prisoners of war. Even when down to ten men Argentina had looked capable of winning. Playing against them has been slow-motion torture, and it seems for ever before Herr Kreitlein's final whistle brings it to a stop. But this release from the discipline – albeit desecrated – of the rules of the game allows a more demonstrative expression of the ill-feeling that has dominated it. The crowd looses off a fusillade of goading boos and sour hisses. Herr Kreitlein spins on his heel and stalks smartly towards the dressing room, but has not got far before he is surrounded by infuriated Argentinian players, soon joined by Lorenzo and his assistants. The barracking turns to jostling, Roberto Ferreira the jostler-in-chief, and by the time he reaches the edge of the pitch Kreitlein has a full police escort to relieve him of the threat of physical assault. Onega spits at Harry Cavan.

Elsewhere, other players abide by the convention that bygones are bygones as soon as a match is completed. Creatures of ritual, they co-operate in the automatic niceties of swapping matey slaps and pats and exchanging shirts. But as the affable George Cohen peels off and prepares to part with his England jersey, Alf Ramsey arrives, running, and grabs it from him. The Argentinian already has one hand on the garment but the England manager shoves him away, tugging at the shirt and barking at an amazed Cohen to get away. It is a public display of passion by Ramsey completely without precedent. Incensed by the dishonourableness, by the whole amorality of Argentina's approach, he is unable to stomach the hypocrisy of a post-match protocol designed to indicate mutual respect. It goes against the grain. He snaps.

Sporadic hostilities continue all the way to the dressing rooms, with Argentinian fists banging on the England door and one player depositing a puddle of urine on the floor outside. Hearing the furore, some of the England men get ready to square up, or make a display of being so at any rate, Big Jack to the fore. It's all gestures in the end. But the rancour is very real. And when Ramsey later makes his way up to the BBC interview room he still cannot contain his rage. The clipped tone is much as usual and the mouth moves with its familiar reluctance, but the eyes can't quite fix his inquisitor with the old studied distance, and one brief passage of speech breaks new ground in candour: 'We have still to produce our best, and this best is not possible until we, ah . . . we meet the right kind of opposition, and that is a team that comes out, ah, to play football and not act as animals, as, ah, we have seen in this World Cup competition.'

The last clause of this assessment may have been a

piece of Ramseyite meaninglessness, or may have been an on-the-verbal-run attempt to make it seem as if he was not referring only to the team England had just defeated. But that is academic. Anyone can tell that the 'animals' he has in mind are Rattin and his colleagues, and the remark strips away the last vestige of pretence that what went on at Wembley today was a contest conducted within a mutually understood code. Rather, it was animated by the protagonists' equal and malign suspicions of each other, driven as much by fear as by valour, and dragged out of the unconscious into the full glare of a clear summer's day in all its compulsive ugliness.

Something similar happens at Hillsborough, the difference being that Uruguay prove themselves less resourceful survivors than Argentina and West Germany more clinical exploiters of the folly of opponents than England. Thirty-six thousand watch referee Jim Finney of England reduce the young South Americans to nine men, starting by dismissing their captain Troche early in the second half after a foul on Emmerich. As a parting gesture, Troche slaps Seeler in the face. Seeler laughs and walks away.

It is as if the Uruguayans have spent the half-time break talking themselves into finding the resolve required to pull back their one-goal arrears, but have forgotten to remind themselves of the equal need for self-control. Eight minutes after Troche's departure Hector Silva goes the same way after the latest of a string of violent Uruguayan infringements against the recalled Haller. Again, English spectators look on, appalled. Again the constabulary step in to prevent ostentatious dissent escalating into open affray.

If frustration was the cause, it wasn't hard to grasp why. In the first seven minutes Uruguay might have scored twice. Firstly, Cortes, a brilliant striker of the ball, smote a breath-taking shot from thirty-five yards that brought a stunning save from Tilkowski, who touched the ball on to the angle before crashing into the post, injuring his head and his left arm. Barely had he recovered when Cortes almost struck again. This time he got his head to a cross, and the save was made by a jumping Schnellinger on the goal-line. The Uruguayans swore that the full-back had parried it with his arm, but Mr Finney tapped his head, West Germany survived and four minutes later took the lead. Held was the scorer after a long shot took a deflection. Mazurkieviez, the Grey Ghost, hadn't a prayer.

The goal filled Uruguay with frustration. The sendings-off now leave them in ruins. West Germany take a grip on the game and eventually squeeze the life out of it. Beckenbauer, who had a frighteningly powerful long shot marvellously saved in the first half, snakes coolly through for West Germany's second. Seeler finds space outside the penalty area on the right and smites a right-foot shot into the top corner with the force of a field gun. Close to the end, Haller shakes off a tackle and glides the fourth with his left foot. Three goals in sixteen minutes. Easy, easy, easy.

*

At Roker Park, the Soviets maintain an immaculate decorum in dooming the Hungarian romance. Gelei the goalkeeper is the tragic figure. Porkujan, retaining his place after taking the honours against Chile, aims a potshot from a short corner. Gelei lets it trundle beneath his body like a goods train going under a tunnel. Chislenko is waiting on the other side to score from a matter of inches. Grateful for this gift, the Soviets defend firmly, break swiftly and almost score again when Malofeev heads against the bar.

Hungary's best effort comes from a free kick by the accomplished defender Sandor Matrai. But, in marked contrast to his opposite number, Lev Yashin saves imperiously, and a minute after the restart the story of the match begins to resemble a tale of two goalkeepers. A Soviet free kick is headed backwards by Meszoly, the one-armed battler in the slaying of Brazil, at the ideal elevation to leave Gelei stranded, denuded, embarrassed. Porkujan picks the cherry.

With nothing to be gained from caution, Hungary stream forward, not just with Albert, Farkas and Bene, but with Sipos, Matrai and the distraught Meszoly too. It is the last of these who finds Bene after a bold run just short of the hour. The winger dips, delays, then hits his shot past Yashin to set the stage for a searing last half-hour. Seven minutes from the end, Sipos smashes a free kick past the Soviet wall and far from Yashin's reach. Or so it seems, until the big man reaches the ball with a huge, stretching dive to tip it away for a corner. There are no more scares. Hungary have proved fatally fallible, the measured Soviets, supreme.

At Goodison Park, all is sensation. Crazy though the events around him were at the time, when Ray Wilson looked up at the Wembley scoreboard to be informed that North Korea were beating Portugal three-nil he was not hallucinating. Taking their cue from the imaginary miniature sidekicks dreamed up by Ken Dodd, the Liverpudlians dub the orientals the 'Diddymen'. It is an affectionate christening, but patronizing. It looks wildly inappropriate as the practice, learning, dedication and comradely optimism of the North Korean players react explosively together in a sublime twenty-five minutes of attacking football which razes Portugal's defence to the ground.

It takes sixty seconds for them to score their first goal and it is a superb one, the culmination of a five-man move. Pak Seung Zin sends his shot in with a zing off the crossbar. For twenty minutes the impact of this freak start sinks in, then the shock is topped up to the point of overflow by two more North Korean goals in sudden succession, both of indisputable quality. Li Dong Woon gets the second and Yang Sung Kook the third. The Portuguese defence is reduced to dyspeptic self-recrimination. The crowd sees things differently: 'We want four!' it demands, half-mad with delight, half-stunned with disbelief. But by half-time reality has rudely interrupted the North Korean fantasy. Eusebio, beside himself with dismay, embarks on a solo rescue mission. He scores quickly with a vicious shot on the turn. Then just before the whistle Torres, who, incredibly, is being contained in the air, is fouled in the penalty area. Eusebio converts with his customary finality. After

153

both goals he follows the ball into the back of the net, tucks it under his arm and jogs back to the centre-spot to hasten the restart. Like Rattin, he is intent on running the game. Unlike Rattin, he intends to do so with pure football genius.

North Korea, thrillingly, keep playing, looking for more goals. The game is an hour old before Portugal draw level then take the lead. Eusebio equalizes with a perfect volley from a cross by Simoes. Then, surging down the left, he breaks three frantic tackles before having his feet sliced from beneath him ten yards out. His fall is heavy and it is three or four minutes before he gets gingerly to his feet, gathers himself for a spot-kick he trusts no one else to take, and leaves Li Chan Myung sprawling.

Four–three, and Eusebio is less a panther than the phoenix of all Portugal. He comes close twice more, then manufactures a fifth goal with a pinpoint corner to Torres, who heads to Augusto, king of the kitchen, who finally heads North Korea out of the World Cup. Nothing, though, can take away their place in football history. Eusebio leaves the field to adulation, and stops to autograph a photograph of him torn from a football magazine proffered in supplication by a little Liverpool boy. Down to the last four, and there are stars in the firmament and blood on the floor. This is football of ultimate intensity, and all human life is here.

Eleven

Monday, 25 July 1966

THERE IS anger on Merseyside. For months Liverpudlians have anticipated that if England reached the semi-
finals they would play at Goodison Park. Everything
everyone has read in the papers, everything they've seen
or heard, has encouraged the impression that the winners of Group One, should they also win their quarter-
final, would be bound for Liverpool. Alas, it has always
been an illusion. The FA's *Official Handbook* makes
explicit that 'the actual allocation of grounds will not
be made until the competing teams are known'. But this
caveat, or at least its likely implication, has not reached
the wider public. Now the announcement has been
made, and pissed off isn't in it.

The primary reason for England versus Portugal
being played at Wembley is, of course, financial. Wembley can expect a full house of close to 100,000 and
takings in the region of £130,000. The same match at
a packed Goodison would yield only half that, which
might not have mattered too much in terms of takings
if the other semi-final had not turned out to be between
West Germany and the 'Russians'. But Londoners who
don't have a ticket already would be unlikely to make

up the numbers alongside agnostic fellow countrymen and 5,000 Germans, some in lederhosen, blowing bull horns. No, England will play Portugal at Wembley and that's that.

The decision suits Alf Ramsey. Going to Goodison would have meant disruption. The England party would have had to move out of the Hendon Hall hotel on the Sunday morning after the bruising bout with Argentina, checked in at Lymm (where the Brazilians stayed) some time in the afternoon, then played the next day against a Portuguese team which would have remained snug as bugs in their beds in Wilmslow. That would never do. And anyway, the Goodison omens were mixed. Contrary to common belief, the first time an England team lost a match on home soil was against the Republic of Ireland, two–nil, at Everton's ground in 1949, a full four years before the 'Magical Magyars' tormented Alf Ramsey and his team mates at Wembley.

The disappointment is reflected in ticket sales. Only 40,000 or so look like coming. There were half as many again for Hungary versus Brazil. Still, there is one compensation, and he arrives in the middle of the afternoon. The Soviet team bus, registration number GNL 704D, pulls up outside Goodison Park and out steps the magnificent figure of Lev Yashin. He has handsome Russian cheekbones and his cigarette-stained teeth do not lessen the impact of his wide, disarming smile. With his brown hair oiled and brushed back from his forehead, he looks like Moscow's answer to a Manhattan swell. On the pavement a delegation meets him with a bunch of carnations and dahlias. Among them is a woman. Yashin steps forward and kisses her directly on the mouth.

Here is the kind of footballer that Liverpool can take to its heart. It helps that he's a goalkeeper. Exactly why goalkeepers enjoy special favour on Merseyside is not easy to say; perhaps they are seen as football's bitter-sweet outsiders, loners lumbered with thankless tasks. But it also helps that Yashin, now thirty-seven, is one of the greatest goalkeepers ever, and that he is honest, intrepid and larger than life. Many goalkeepers now wear all-black kit, but with Yashin it is a trademark, integral to his charisma. When play is far away, Yashin strides about his goalmouth like a restless giant. When it threatens, he commands his area mightily, his mere presence a deterrent. When he makes a save he displays a magisterial athleticism, his large limbs and enormous hands devouring everything. The 'Black Octopus' they call him back home.

Home is the Moscow Dynamo club, famous not only for its football but also for its association with the KGB. Yashin, though, fits into a different idea about what a Russian might be, something far more human and romantic. Perhaps, deep down, this owes something to the desperate Soviet resistance to Hitler's armies, little more than twenty years in the past. Perhaps, too, it owes a little to local knowledge. Some Liverpudlians have encountered real live Russians among the cornucopia of visiting seafarers. In Bootle, for example, Soviet sailors sometimes disembark and play impromptu games of football on the shore, watched by little groups of fascinated locals.

Yashin aside, though, the Soviet team is still regarded as anonymous. This is partly because it has been insulated from the mechanisms of personality creation, and partly because the operators of these mechanisms don't believe that the Soviet players have personalities to create. In other words, journalists find them hard to communicate with – cultural suspicions, language problems and so on – and aren't much inclined to persevere because they believe it will be a waste of effort. For these reasons the 'Russians' have an image problem which is rooted in a self-fulfilling prophecy and does not do justice to their exploits on the field of play. While it is true that they've been organized and muscular, the men in the red shirts with the inscription 'CCCP' – 'USSR' in Russia's Cyrillic script – have also displayed subtlety and skill. Although the blunders of Hungary's goalkeeper made the difference in their quarter-final, the skills of Chislenko and Sabo were more evident on that occasion than those of Florian Albert. Valeriy Voronin has shown himself to be a bit of a maestro in either defence or midfield. Yet the men from the far side of the Iron Curtain would have to walk from their dressing room wearing tutus and high heels to shed their reputation for being durable, dull and dour.

The West Germans might make a similar complaint. Like their opponents they are stuck with a reputation which doesn't square with their talents or their contribution to the World Cup so far. They've negotiated an exacting path – far more exacting than England's – with fortitude, skill and better grace than many. Against the Swiss they were stupendous, against Argentina they were tough but restrained. They outlasted the Spanish. Uruguay, they first outnerved and then demolished. In the course of those five games West Germany have emerged as major contenders. Established heavyweights like Seeler and Schnellinger have been joined by others: the smooth Haller, the lightning Held, the immaculate sweeper Willi Schulz and the multi-talented Beckenbauer.

For these reasons, West Germany go into the match as favourites. But because they are the favourites, because of Yashin, because anti-German feeling is a great British tradition and, just maybe, because there's a bit of scouse devilment to be had from supporting the Red Menace, especially after FIFA's perceived snub, the Liverpudlian neutrals side with the Soviets. Even as Yashin warms up, they shout the goalkeeper's name. And there he is in the flesh, looking massive in his baggy shorts and v-necked keeper's sweater with his right leg bandaged. But there's also a counter-cry: 'U-we! U-we!' Flags of red, black and yellow wave in adoration of the West Germans' dauntless number 9. It's a clash of the indestructibles.

Yashin is called into action right at the start. Seeler is fouled thirty yards from his goal, and Emmerich swings his sledgehammer left foot at the free kick. Yashin takes off across his goal with balletic power and clasps the ball with both hands. Then the heavy body contact starts. West Germany make the early running and the USSR get nervous. Beckenbauer sets off on one of his spectral excursions into his opponents' heartland. He's looking up, measuring the distance for a pass or a

shot, when Sabo swoops from the side and fouls him
with a trip that is as blatant as it is dangerous. There
is, though, a rough justice in the outcome of this assault.
For while Beckenbauer stays suavely upright, Sabo ends
up in an agonized heap. After treatment, he hobbles
helplessly to the wing and proceeds to contribute fitfully
with one leg only. Ten minutes gone and the Soviets,
through a lack of the very discipline with which they
are assumed to be chillingly indoctrinated, are effectively down to ten men.

It's all hard running, thumping tackles and breathless
battles for space. It's a tactical contest, too. The West
Germans, in white shirts with black trim, play in a
novel, diamond-shaped formation. In front of Tilkowski, Schulz sweeps and Friedel Lutz (replacing Horst
Höttges), Weber and Schnellinger man-mark the Soviet
forwards, though the latter has both the freedom and
the ability to go forward down the flanks. Beckenbauer
is the spine of the team, its central nervous system.
Overath stabilizes and hits long balls with a left foot he
could open a can of peaches with. Haller roams along
the right side, augmenting the attack. Emmerich sticks
to the left, a mobile cannon. Held is everywhere. Seeler
is a bag of nails.

The USSR, though, stick to their task with determination and an intelligence that is, in part, unscrupulous.
While Voronin marshals the defence and the big forwards, Banishevskiy and Malofeev, strive gamely to
push and pull their captors out of position, some in the
crowd have been watching Sabo off the ball. Almost
useless as a player, the most valuable service he seems

to think he can provide is to render one of the Germans useless too. Every time a player in a white shirt comes near, Sabo seems to try to kick him out of the match. It's as 'professional' as that. But there's kicking going on all over the pitch. Haller is cropped. Beckenbauer is cropped. Beckenbauer crops someone else. Voronin and Beckenbauer are booked, the West German for the second time in the competition. Seeler is a perpetual handful, barging, tumbling, bouncing back. Yashin has to throw himself into a ruck with Seeler and Emmerich and three of his own side. He emerges, unperturbed, with the ball.

But two minutes before half-time the Soviet resistance sustains a double dose of damage. Chislenko, half-forward, loses the ball to an iron Schnellinger crash-tackle which leaves him prone. It's not a foul, and Schnellinger surges into the vacuum where Sabo might have been. He spots Haller, circling, twenty-five yards ahead and aims a low pass towards him. When the ball leaves his boot it seems a hopeful effort, over-ambitious. When it reaches its target, it is seen to be wholly perfect. The ball runs past Haller to his right, leaving his marker to his left turning and losing ground. Haller adjusts to the course of the ball, overhauls it, plants his left foot down, pivots, and hammers a waist-high shot just inside the Soviets' left-hand post. Yashin dives, in vain.

As the West Germans celebrate, Chislenko is treated at the sideline following Schnellinger's tackle. He's seemed irate for much of the game and now he's in a fury. Unwisely, the Soviet benchmen let him back on before half-time, or maybe he just ignores an instruction to stay. Hobbling, he receives the ball, loses it, then aims an angry kick at Held right under the nose of Concetto Lo Bello, the Italian referee. Mr Lo Bello points to the dressing room. Barely has Chislenko come back on than he is off for good. Seconds later the half-time whistle blows and he is joined by his shattered team mates. Semi-finals are about self-control as much as anything else. The Soviets have lost theirs badly and they've paid a dreadful price.

It's near enough eleven against nine for the second period. The USSR defend bravely and even muster a shot or two. But after sixty-eight minutes the West Germans at last capitalize on their advantage. Beckenbauer glides decoratively around a tackle and sets himself from twenty yards. As he steals a glance at the goal, defenders are closing in, but he has the measure of every fragment of a second and every inch of Yashin's goal. He strikes the ball with his left foot. It flies, curving in the air. Where's Yashin? He moves across. The ball flies on. Yashin watches it as it snakes inside his right-hand post. He doesn't even dive. Could he have reached it? Should he have? Is it possible that the great man has made a fatal misjudgement in one of the biggest games of his life?

Incredibly, his depleted team perseveres. There's a general belief that Tilkowski is uncomfortable coming for crosses. A shot from an angle has him diving, and he stays down, holding his shoulder. Recovered – or seemingly so – from his second injury in two games, he resumes and the Soviets continue to press. With three minutes to go a high ball into the centre from Voronin has Tilkowski in a flap. He drops it and Porkujan taps in to make the score two–one. But extra time is too much to hope for, and for the third time in five matches West Germany have defeated opposition depleted by sendings-off. But not getting sent off is all part of the game. The West Germans have looked a little edgy but still hugely able. As the final whistle of their last World Cup game blows, the Goodison Park crowd take up a new chant: 'ENG-LAND! ENG-LAND!' Whether inspired by patriotism, sarcasm or just a little of both is difficult to tell. Whatever, the West Germans have their place in the final. Beckenbauer walks away coolly. Yashin smiles, embraces Tilkowski, and takes his sad leaving of Liverpool.

Twelve

Tuesday, 26 July 1966

THE SECOND semi-final kicks off. Everyone is watching Eusebio, especially Nobby Stiles. For three days the meeting of the two has been billed as the decisive contest within a contest, and as press and public interest has snowballed, so the two protagonists have been elevated into symbolic figures, as if mystical representatives of their respective races and nations: Eusebio, the Black Panther, the magic man from Mozambique; Stiles, the English anti-hero, a Tommy Atkins figure whose toothlessness creates an impression of ferocity and innocence at once. Both are hugely conscious of the attention their exploits have focused on them. In the space of a fortnight their lives, already exceptional, have changed for ever more.

Eusebio is now unassailable as the World Cup's most brilliant individual. In every game he has shone and in all but the first he has scored. He has eclipsed the great Pele and parted the Brazilians from the Jules Rimet trophy. He has saved his country from humiliation by North Korea. He is elemental, inexplicable, almost extraterrestrial. When his team left the Stanneylands Hotel there were crowds of fans to see them off and lots of disappointed girls, but the send-off was cosy, with handshakes for the staff and mementoes for the local journalists. But since they've arrived in London the madness has multiplied ten times. The media are massed everywhere and so are soccer's entrepreneurs. Agents from Juventus and both the Madrid teams, Real and Athletico, have been making overtures. But Internazionale, the richest of all, have offered Benfica £250,000 and Eusebio himself £100,000 to join them in Milan. Eusebio is flattered. He's going to think it over. But first there's Stiles to contend with.

Stiles will get paid sixty quid to mark Eusebio for England, the same fee as everyone else. Not that he's bothered about money. As ever, he's got a point to make. He has seen a quote which has Eusebio saying he hopes the referee will make sure Stiles doesn't kick him to death. Stiles knows that Eusebio probably never said it, but he quite likes the idea that he did, because it would mean that Eusebio is nervous. And Stiles believes Eusebio would have a reason for being so. The two players have never competed in an international together before, but in March they met twice at club level in the quarter-final of the European Cup. Manchester United beat Benfica in the first leg at Old Trafford, but only by three goals to two, leaving them vulnerable in the return match at Lisbon's spectacular Stadio da Luz – the Stadium of Light – in front of 80,000 people. Before the kick-off in the shadow of the Benfica eagle, Eusebio was officially presented with his award of European Footballer of the Year and went on a lap of honour before his adoring fans. Yet the occasion inspired a Manchester miracle. Within fifteen minutes they were three goals up, two scored brilliantly by George Best (whom the Portuguese press christened El Beatle), the third by John Connelly. Bobby Charlton embroidered United's final goal at the death to complete a stunning five–one win. In both matches, Stiles had marked Eusebio and restricted him severely.

Yet Stiles cannot hope to contain him for every second, and a very few uncontained seconds may be all Eusebio requires to complete a demolition. As the play takes shape, it emerges that England's plan to curb him does not require Stiles to go for him man-to-man, but for the whole defence to block him collectively, and the rest of the Portuguese forward line as well. It is a strategy founded on confidence in Gordon Banks. The England goalkeeper is so good, so invulnerable to error, that not even Eusebio is likely to beat him from thirty yards. The trick, then, is to keep Eusebio at that distance. It means defending in depth and with unerring compactness, obliging Eusebio to retreat, forcing him to pass sideways, distancing him from his sidekick Torres and giving him no room to rampage. The construction of this stern fortress frees Stiles to patrol its outer walls and harass any who threaten. The result is he's not exactly inside Eusebio's shorts but he's always hovering at their hem, a worry, a pest, a little granite gnat.

There's a great warmth about the occasion, despite the numbing effect on every nerve of so much being at stake. Ball feels a knot of fear in his stomach, and he welcomes it because it tells him he is ready to go out

and get something he really, really wants. But the mal-
odour of the Argentina match has been dispersed by a
fragrance of hope and pleasure. It's rather different in
Buenos Aires, where the newspapers have snarled
unpleasantly of 'English Pirates' and 'Secret Pact
Between England and Germany', and have threatened
darkly to invade the disputed Falkland Islands. FIFA,
however, has fined the Argentinians one thousand Swiss
francs – the maximum permitted – suspended Rattin
for the next four internationals and Ferreira and
Onega for the next three. It has also censured Ramsey
for what he said in his television interview. Mr Alan
Scott, honorary secretary of the Dog Owners' Association, was also displeased by the reference to 'animals'.
He said: 'May I immediately disassociate the dog world
from this description as being most unfair to our many
members and their pets who insist on control at all
times.'

On this day, as their compatriots on the pitch edge
towards composure, the England supporters exude the
more attractive manifestations of national self-esteem.
The English character on display today is generous and
relaxed, satisfied by the qualities that have enabled its
team to get this far and equally ready to appreciate the
different virtues of others. To have reached the semi-
final means England have escaped the last threat of
disgrace: if they lose today they can safely claim that
no one has been let down. The Portuguese, meanwhile,
are seen as offering a noble challenge rather than a vile
threat. The punishment Morais meted out to Pelé has
not disfigured their image as the tournament's premier

purveyors of pure entertainment (and he's been left out of the side today anyway). The task of the English is defined in its supporters' minds as getting the measure of them by means that are just as admirable and just as much their own. The men in white shirts are seen to personify a quite different England to that which used to be symbolized by its football stars. Rather than a place of fearless free spirits of the type that conquered half the world, the England of the Charlton brothers, Stiles and Moore adds up to another version, freshly formed on the playing field of the national imagination, a place where honesty, selflessness, courage and decency are stoutly marshalled to resist rivals whom nature has endowed with greater gifts.

The England players have anticipated the Portugal game in much the same way. To them, the attitude of Argentina was nothing less than profane, their games-manship sheer dishonourableness, their brand of pro-fessionalism the lowest form of skulduggery. Their ample skills were seen as grotesquely wasted and their refusal to try and win by straightforward attack as cowardly, almost a failure of manhood. But England like the Portuguese. The two matches they played against them in 1964 were attractive and disputed fairly. Since then, if they've spotted the Portuguese team coach or bumped into the players at airports there have been exchanges of waves and shakes of hands. But the England team also like the Portuguese because they expect to defeat them. Having reached the last four and scraped past Argentina, they have anticipated the

169

Portugal game buoyed up by a combination of confidence and relief.

It shows in all parts of their game. The watchfulness demanded by the presence of Simoes, Torres and Eusebio has a lighter underside which the enterprise of Portugal enables England to liberate at last. Although they have four men covering the midfield, all bar Stiles yearn to burst forward. Against Portugal's 4–3–3, Peters, Ball and Bobby Charlton at last enjoy the freedom to parade their best skills, especially Charlton. Aside from his goal against Mexico and a few other scattered moments, he has seemed inhibited, out of sorts. Off the field he's a shy man, one of the squad's heavier smokers, often pensive and withdrawn, not like his brash big brother at all. Some mistake his diffidence for surliness but its true root lies in modesty and deep reserve. This part of his character is replicated on the field if he makes an error, when his whole body seems embarrassed and ashamed. But today Bobby Charlton has a look of joy about him as he sweeps long passes to his team mates or just canters off the ball. It seems to infect the entire England team, perhaps Portugal's as well. Even in the early nervous stages, the game flows. It is twenty-three minutes before Pierre Schwinte of France blows his whistle for a foul.

Upfront for England, Hurst and Hunt forage the more keenly because of Portugal's determination to do the same. They will never be like Eusebio. They will never be like Jimmy Greaves, sitting with the reserves, knowing his stitches are healing but with no way of knowing if he will get back in the team should it advance to the final. But their selflessness and application have their own kind of appeal: Hurst, controlling the ball however it comes to him; Hunt pounding the pitch as much for others as for himself. Sir Roger has plenty of newspaper critics who put half a dozen other English forwards ahead of him in their personal orders of merit. But his England team mates love him, and after half an hour he shows everybody watching why.

Wilson, with the peripatetic Simoes in his eyeline only from time to time, takes the chance to display his range. Looking up, nudging the ball to where his left foot can use it best, he strikes a long pass towards the D of the far penalty box and into the path of Hunt's stooped sprint between two Portuguese. It's a beautiful ball, placed to the inch, though still hard to control first time on the run. Hunt can't do it, but his touch takes the ball past his nearest challenger and on towards Pereira in goal. Pereira is good, but he's looked a bit spooked today. Now, without warning, he must rush from his goal-line at the feet of the England striker. He makes the dash but more in panic than out of resolution. Instead of smothering the ball with body and hands, he blocks it away with his ankles. It rebounds along the ground, back past the advancing Hunt, over the eighteen-yard line and directly into the path of Bobby Charlton.

Pereira is prostrate, his defence is scattered, there is no one covering on his line. Behind him, the net awaits. The eruption of sound provoked by Hunt's run abates a fraction and in this millisecond Charlton makes a decision. He could blast it, knee over the ball, foot tilted downwards like a dancer's and *whack*. Instead, his instinct tells him to place it, use the inside of the foot and deliver an emphatic but controlled strike. Pereira, barely back on his feet, turns to watch the ball billow the bottom of the net and Charlton stretches his arms to the sky. It's a moment of vindication and also part of a bigger mystery. Charlton is repaying the faith of a public that has been yearning for him to bloom. But the goal is also the culmination of his entire contribution to the match so far, and that cannot be explained only by the openness of the Portuguese. Today, Charlton's long passes are finding their targets, the poise, the balance, the sense of purpose are all there. Ramsey's detractors have always claimed that he plays too safe. But moving Bobby Charlton from the wing to become his team's creative wellspring is a continuing calculated risk. No one suggests that Charlton lacks appetite, but sometimes, as with Greaves, the juices just don't flow. Today they do. Lucky England. Lucky, because there is no legislating for how Charlton is performing today, for what footballers call 'form'.

Both teams now face unfamiliar situations. England are playing well. Can it last? Portugal are confronted with a side that looks capable of holding them at bay. This switch of roles puts new demands on both sets of players, but the greater urgency falls to the Portuguese, a goal down against an England that is suddenly fluent and in its own backyard. They strive to hit back. Eusebio has been crowded but he cannot be crushed. He's already struck a drive that was deflected wide, but only by a foot. Now Augusto floats a centre towards Torres.

Big Jack Charlton, three inches shorter, wins it but cannot control where it goes. The ball dollies up, then begins to drop, falling towards the corner of the box in the direction of Eusebio, who fixes it in his sight. It's going to fall on top of him if he stays where he is. So he shunts backwards one step, then two, eyes almost popping with anticipation, setting himself, then right foot back to lash the ball at goal before it has the chance to bounce.

It's a scoring chance, but the sort the ordinary player would sooner do without. The quality of co-ordination demanded between eye and foot is frighteningly high. It's the kind of opportunity which, if accepted, usually results in exercise for the ballboys and a whoop of derision from the crowd. Eusebio, though, shapes faultlessly and strikes the falling ball past three white shirts looming towards him. It's truly hit and heads at speed to the right of Banks who throws himself, can't catch it, but does just enough. The ball ricochets off his arms and chest, runs loose and Stiles sweeps it behind, then turns, raging at his own team mates. Bawling, his arm flies upwards, his head juts forwards and his body kinks in the middle with the force of his fury. It's Wilson he's angriest with, and Wilson bawls back, breaking off only to take up his position for Eusebio's corner-kick. The crowd chants: 'NOBBY STILES! NOBBY STILES!'

England's lead lasts until the interval. After that Portugal come at them again, but the defence still holds. Cohen, with his sloping shoulders and prosaic skills, is a rock at right-back. Jack Charlton, looking up at Torres, holds his own. Bobby Moore is simply imperial, cover-

173

ing, organizing, taking the ball away from the danger men with absolute assurance and style, and turning defence into attacks of a grace and imagination England have seemed incapable of before. At one point Ball and Stiles, colluding down the right, lose communication and give away a throw. First they shout at each other. Then they laugh. Steadily, as the half wears on, England regain the initiative. Bobby Charlton maintains his influence. In the crowd, voices are raised every time he's in possession: 'Go on, Bobby, go on!' Ball seems to be everywhere, joining the attack, tackling back, and with eleven minutes to go he's out on the left stroking a pass inside to Moore just short of halfway.

Moore swivels and slides the ball with grooved deliberation down to Cohen on the right touchline. Cohen, bustling, looks up and hits it long towards the last Portuguese defender, José Carlos. It drifts into the penalty area and Carlos seems content to shepherd it out of play, but it doesn't run and Pereira doesn't come, and Hurst bears down on him. He's inside Carlos, shakes free of him and drags the ball back into space. Again, there's one of those tiny moments when everything seems to stop still and possibilities turn into probabilities. Hurst, in his fashion, has done the hard work. Now he needs composure. He holds the ball, one touch, two, then rolls it gently back in the direction of his own goal. From sixteen yards Bobby Charlton shoots first time with such force that he leaves the ground with the recoil. The hard slap of the ball against the net is matched in conviction only by the crowd's great jump to attention as it joins Charlton in celebration.

As Charlton runs back to the centre-spot the Portuguese he passes hold out their hands to congratulate him. It's been an exceptionally sporting game, almost unreal compared with so much of what's gone before, yet surely these are also the handshakes of resignation. Portugal is on the brink, England can barely begin to contain its excitement. The crowd chants: 'We want three!' It sings: 'Oh when the whites go marching in!' But it's not all over. Portugal throw everything forward and Torres escapes his jailers Jack Charlton and Banks to head towards a vacant goal. Big Jack does the professional thing: he knocks it away with his hand and walks off in dismay. It's a penalty and England's clean sheet seems certain to be besmirched.

Eusebio plants the ball on the spot. He's scored three from there already *en route* to this great Wembley day and each has been scored the same way: hard and waist-high to the goalkeeper's right. Not textbook, but crushingly effective. Banks knows this, of course he does, and he's prepared. But Coluna has a word in Eusebio's ear and Banks spots it. As Eusebio runs up, Banks decides to risk second-guessing him. He moves to his left. Eusebio hits it to his right: same pace, same place, same result. The force of the shot is so great that the ball rebounds all the way from the net back over the goal-line where Eusebio, as against North Korea, fields it and turns to run back for the restart. Banks is kicking himself. Eusebio pauses to touch him consolingly on the cheek. Two–one.

Union Jacks are waving everywhere still, but there's a crackle of anxiety which builds into a full-scale emergency as Simoes takes possession a few yards out, sets himself and looks sure to equalize. Out of nowhere, Stiles appears and whips the ball away. Make that Saint Stiles. Then Coluna, so suave throughout, sends a harsh drive towards Banks's goal which the England keeper tips over almost serenely. Five matches, now, and not one mistake from the former coal-delivery man in the yellow jersey. Letting in a Eusebio penalty does not qualify. And now it doesn't matter as the match comes to an end, and Portugal's swashbuckling advance is halted.

The two teams form up to honour the Portuguese dignitaries, guests in the royal box. Eusebio's face begins to crumple and, as the lines break up, he embraces Bobby Charlton, then hurries away, mopping his tears with his shirt. In the England dressing room Alf Ramsey calls for silence and declares that, gentlemen, we surely all agree that Nobby turned in a very professional performance today. Across the corridor Eusebio weeps, as the England players give Saint Nobby a big round of applause.

Thirteen

Saturday, 30 July 1966

ENGLAND MAY not win the final, but for some the 8th World Cup has already been a victory. In their White City offices, the World Cup Organization team can congratulate themselves on a job well done. Assuming a full house for the final game at Wembley, 1,614,677 tickets for places will have been bought for the thirty-two World Cup matches at a total cost of £1,551,099 13s 6d. Nearly 80 per cent of the total places available at the eight World Cup venues have been taken up, which, given the complexities of the season-ticket system, is almost as near to a sell-out as it was possible to get. They're also pretty pleased up the road from Shepherd's Bush at BBC TV Centre. The unprecedented live coverage, especially in evening prime time, has brought a number of complaints, but few are carping now. The incredible figure of 400 million people from around the world are expected to be watching the final today. And since England's participation means it is a great day for the entire nation, a certain peripheral individual is seeking to get in on the act too.

The BBC's Bryan Cowgill gets wind of this when he receives an unexpected visit from a minion of Harold

Wilson. The Prime Minister has been to the United States, where he has discussed Britain's insane economic situation with President Johnson, but he's made sure to be back for the final. His 'reserved' ticket is already on his royal box seat, two places from the Queen's. All perfectly proper. But now his eager aide has a suggestion to make. Would it be possible to arrange for the PM to be interviewed at half-time? Maybe to pass an observation on the progress of the game? That might be difficult, responds Cowgill, breaking this unhappy news as gently as he can. Very well: then after the match, perhaps? enquires the aide. Bit tricky really, explains Cowgill, hedging with a poise his supplicant's master would admire. Can't really foresee how things might end up, you see. Thanks just he same.

Elsewhere, another national figure endures an infinitely deeper disappointment. At Hendon Hall Ramsey announces to his squad that England will be represented in the final by the same team that started against Portugal. Banks, Moore, the Charltons, Stiles and probably Wilson and Cohen must have been sure of their positions, Peters and Ball less so. Hurst and Hunt would have been rigid with fear if Ramsey hadn't told them their good news in strict confidence the day before, hoping to improve their chances of getting a good night's sleep. But for Jimmy Greaves, fit again, it's the first he's heard that he isn't going to play. It's a shattering blow. He finds a few brave words, but cannot put on a face to go with them. As the squad clambers into the team coach, he looks exactly what he is: a very sad man indeed.

Ramsey has been in agony with the Greaves dilemma. Fate has handed him a choice between leaving England's greatest goalscorer out of England's first ever World Cup final, or sacrificing one of Hunt or Hurst, the two men whose goals dragged England out of the slough in earlier games, and who combined well against Portugal. His decision to stick with his winning team will earn him no praise in the history books if England fail. But perhaps he has taken strength from the tidal wave of approval which has swollen up from nowhere since the semi-final win. Just as Moore, Bobby Charlton and Stiles have been lifted on to pedestals, he too has been transformed in the popular consciousness from a prickly pragmatist into a master thinker, the man with the plan, a soccer messiah leading the great game's inventors back from their years in the wilderness to the brink of global domination again.

Simply, nothing else matters in England today. Not the public spending cuts, not the run on the pound, not the war in Vietnam, not the Rolling Stones, not Twiggy, not LSD. It's absurd, but there it is. Only Alf Ramsey, the enigma from Dagenham with the strained enunciation and the brittle public manner, is of the slightest interest: he and his brave England team. They arrive at Wembley Stadium to find the greatest tumult in the capital since VE Day twenty-one years before. It isn't polite to mention it, of course, and many haven't even thought about it, but there is no mistaking that the public's edge of anticipation is the keener because the other team are Germans. A certain smug disdain for 'Krauts', for 'Jerries', for 'Huns', for the 'Boche', runs deep in the culture. Yet there is also a certain ambivalence. Commentators deem that the English football character is similar to that of the Germans: hard but honest, physical but clean, according to such as *The Times*'s Geoffrey Green. But the acknowledgement of likeness also seems to require qualifying by means of a dip back into the mythology of English football's past, just to emphasize our separateness and – whisper it – our superiority. The Germans are coldly efficient. We are burningly resolute. They are cybernauts. We are human beings.

In truth, though, West Germany's team have been almost as solid in defence as England's (conceding just two goals against England's one) and a lot more expansive in attack. They have also come through against four strong opponents in their five games, twice as many as England, and have scored thirteen goals in the process compared with England's seven. Except for the semi-final against the USSR, they have also performed at every stage with rather more *élan*. And they, like England, seem superbly conditioned. Despite the final being at Wembley, their boisterous supporters are filling large patches of the stadium with their flags and blaring klaxons. They have reason for confidence. Anything can happen out there. It's the final, a one-off, and West Germany is prepared.

The England players know this too. But they still fancy their chances. Young Beckenbauer, it is generally agreed, has been a surprise star of the tournament and plays despite being twice booked, thanks to a FIFA dispensation. Willi Schulz, the gaunt sweeper, seems imperturbable. But Seeler, some have decided, is past his best. Emmerich has got only one good foot. Tilkowski can't catch. Haller has been hosannaed, but Stiles thinks he hurdles tackles and is too fat, and there are mutterings that he's a bit of an actor. Hunt has encountered Weber for Liverpool against Cologne: he's good but not that good. Ball decides that if Schnellinger is going to keep tabs on him from start to finish he'll have to be the fittest man alive. And England have never been beaten by West Germany, not once, not anywhere.

England know how to go about the job, too. The West Germans don't defend in retreating layers like Argentina but they man-mark rigorously, with Schulz clearing up the loose ends. The secret will be to get around the sweeper's broom. That means Hunt and Hurst, supported by Ball, running their studs off even when the ball is far away from them, dragging their markers around to leave gaps for others to move into. Peters and, in particular, Bobby Charlton will be vitally important there. But everyone should be looking to use their initiative. If there's a chance to advance, take it, because someone else will have worked to create that chance. To beat the West Germans England need to be flexible and persistent and to play for each other all day. They ought to manage that: it's what they're best at.

In the dressing room, it's bedlam until well after two o'clock. The place seems to be full of pressmen, camera crews and bureaucrats. Slowly, they thin out, leaving the manager, trainers, players and the reserves: Eastham chattering, Springett joking, Hunter with his raincoat,

Armfield in an equally habitual red sweater and a black
polo-necked jumper – and he's not a bit superstitious.
Greaves is in a blazer and tie, looking a bit sick. He
does his best not to cast a pall. He wishes Hunt and all
the rest the best of luck. Because of a direct clash with
their opponents' kit, England's shirts are red, their
shorts white. Stiles goes through his usual arcane pal-
aver with the shirt and the boots, the Vaseline and olive
oil, the eyes and teeth. Ball, Banks and Wilson mess
about. Cohen gets on with it, amiably. Next to Moore,
Jack Charlton falls quiet. He and his brother's parents
came in to the hotel this morning to wish them luck.
The younger Charlton and Hunt are pensive. Hurst and
Peters might just be wondering if they're about to wake
up. Two weeks ago they had five England caps between
them. Now they're about to play in the World Cup
final. Ramsey says no more than usual: gentlemen, we
can't let these people beat us today, can we? Not these
Germans. There's a look in his eye. He really wants that
prize.

In the tunnel Weber and Overath of Cologne and
Emmerich Tilkowski and Held of Borussia Dortmund
wish Hunt, their old opponent, good luck. Hunt stands
behind Banks, who stands behind Ball, behind Cohen,
behind Moore at the front. Behind Hunt, it's Wilson,
Hurst, Bobby Charlton, Peters, Stiles and, as ever, Jack
Charlton. Ten minutes before kick-off. Clack-clack,
they click their feet on the tunnel's concrete floor. Then,
as the two files, the red and the white, start their walk
towards the green and the light they become more
aware of the gurgle of noise which rises to a torrent as

they come into the view of the crowd. There's no pattern to it at first. It's just a great, bank-bursting flood of cheering and clapping and rattling, and cries of 'ENGLAND!' and the klaxons of the West German supporters, and their flags waving defiantly among the proliferating Union Jacks and occasional crosses of St George.

The England team have become more than a group of professional sportsmen. They are players on a bigger stage, the stage of public passion and popular sentiment. In the space of twenty days, millions have invested a bit of their heart in the efforts of Banks, Ball, Stiles, Moore, the Charlton boys. It's only football, for God's sake. But it's also an expression of common sentiment and an unprecedented manifestation of a relationship between footballers and their fans which is changing, and looks bound to change completely as big-time football becomes less of a folk culture and more of a commodity and the players move out of the homes they rent from their clubs for a pound or so a week and start buying bungalows in the suburbs and filling them with cocktail cabinets and radiograms. But for now, even on a day as big as this when the stars are under a spotlight as bright as any at the London Palladium, the England players are still touchable, recognizable, still just about the kinds of men who might live next door to a plumber, a plasterer or a lorry driver, still people you might see walking down the same streets as you.

Yesterday, room mates Ray Wilson and Bobby Charlton went shopping in Hendon, just the two of them alone. Like everyone else, they were desperately restless. It was something to do. They could hardly move for well-wishers, ordinary people who knew that they – especially that nice Bobby Charlton – were a bit special, but felt that the distance between them could be easily bridged. And it was bridged with something that felt very much like friendship. So there they were, two northern boys, born into postwar austerity, who grew up in mining villages, now killing time in the bland shopping stores of the London outskirts, and finding that everybody knew their names. It felt strange, almost shocking. But it also felt warm and right.

The two teams line up for the national anthems looking up at the royal box. The band of the Royal Marines plays 'God Save the Queen' and 'Deutschland Über Alles'. There's the Queen herself, doing her duty, feigning interest. There's her husband, the Duke. They are mysteries, enigmas. When they appeared in their places, the crowd craned their necks for a glimpse. Flanking them are Sir Stanley Rous and the Earl of Harewood, FA president. There's Harold Wilson having genial words with his Economic Affairs Secretary George Brown and his Chancellor James Callaghan, the first the three of them have exchanged for a week or two during which they have argued furiously about the economy. Also well clear of the cheap seats is world heavyweight boxing champion Cassius Clay, here to defend his title against 'Our 'Enry', Henry Cooper. People are learning that they must now call Clay 'Muhammad Ali' instead. Something to do with becoming a Muslim. All very strange. Also in the crowd is Eusebio in a blue raincoat, looking wistful. Still, he has his consolations. He is sure to end up as the tournament's leading scorer and will be given the Golden Boot award for his pains. He got his ninth – another penalty – during Portugal's two–one defeat of the Soviet Union in the meaningless Third and Fourth Place final (Torres got the other, Malofeev replying) and was cheered off the field.

That was on Thursday evening. Since then it has rained almost constantly. The pitch is green and slippery and the white lines wet. In the centre-circle Moore and Seeler conduct the usual preliminaries. Seeler played his first international against England on this ground in 1954 when he was just eighteen. Matthews, Wright and Finney played for England (Ramsey had only just bowed out of internationals after the drubbing by Hungary the previous year) and West Germany were the holders of the Jules Rimet trophy. In the centre-circle Moore shakes his hand, swaps pennants, exchanges pleasantries. The referee is the Swiss, Gottfried Dienst, a dapper, fastidious figure, his black hair brushed up into neat waves. His linesmen are Dr Karol Galba of Czechoslovakia and Tofik Bakhramov the Azerbaijani from the Soviet Union. Bakhramov is an eccentric figure: tall and stringy with long shorts, grey hair, a dark moustache and a thin white belt hanging loosely round his waist.

Dienst offers a coin for the captains' inspection, flips it and Moore wins. He opts to keep his team at the same end, signals to Seeler and jogs away, stretching his back muscles, blowing out phlegm. The teams form up. The West Germans have kick-off. There's a great white

185

blot on the ball from the damp centre spot. Dienst blows. Held taps the ball to Overath, who stops it, steps back and curls a pass out to the right wing to where Haller might have been if he'd been a greyhound. Throw-in to England. The final is under way.

The players strive to acclimatize. They're not novices at coping with big-match stress, but today they are writing history as they go along. A football match is a human drama with all the uncertainties that implies, composed on the run by each one of its players. Eleven individuals co-operate, more or less effectively, in imposing a script to their own liking upon eleven others seeking to do the same. There are possibilities, probabilities, but nothing is preordained. None can legislate for the role of luck or the vagaries of touch, mood or form. But Alf Ramsey has made his reputation by cramping the style of chance. He's got closer than most to bringing ninety minutes of sweating, shoving, shouting and immense athletic eloquence under some degree of control. He's done it his own way too, deliberately, single-mindedly. His players have always responded. Now they have to show the world what it's all been worth.

One minute. Höttges, back in place of Lutz, fouls Hurst from behind. The English supporters boo, getting the tension off their chests. Wilson takes the kick, finds Bobby Charlton, who feeds Stiles coming forward into space. Yes. That's Stiles, coming forward into space. His shot is blocked and the rebound reaches Cohen. The ball skims off his heel and behind him, high and not very handsome.

Two minutes. The first clear chance of the match falls to Sigi Held. Emmerich chips it to him, hovering in a gap between Moore and Jack Charlton. He brings it down on his chest and spins. He's on his own, twelve yards out, and this could be a sensation. Heart in mouth Held snatches at his shot and hoiks it weakly wide.

Nerves, nerves, and muscles overwound. The pitch is big and slippery. At this early stage and in such circumstances, every player is frail.

As Banks walks backwards to take the first restart kick of the match, the trigonometry of the afternoon is laid out on the field. As expected, the West Germans mark man-to-man and, again as expected, Höttges sticks to Hurst, Weber to Hunt and Schnellinger to Ball. Less predictable, though, is the proximity of Beckenbauer to Bobby Charlton. For the next few minutes the opposing players, in that curious complicity of competitive team games, get on with getting to know each other. They test each other, locating boundaries, exploring avenues. If I go there, will he follow? If I try this, will he do that? The England formation displays its flexibility. Hurst drops very deep and pulls very wide to the left. Bobby Charlton appears on the touchlines, Ball pops up on the left, the blond Schnellinger in tow.

Six minutes. Slowly, the players begin to get a grip. Stiles tackles Beckenbauer, tersely and well. West Germany win the first corner, but it comes to nothing. Stiles comes forward again and crosses towards Hunt. It's a ploy: give Tilkowski a high one to test his fitness and jangle his nerves. Tilkowski punches. It falls to Bobby Charlton, who lobs it back towards the keeper, allowing him no rest. As he jumps, Hurst clatters into him, roughing him up. Tilkowski falls and lands in a heap, hurt yet again. Play continues as Ball scraps madly for the ball on the edge of the box, with the West German goal vacant. But Dienst blows for a free kick against him. The West German trainer comes on with a bucket and sponge. Tilkowski gets to his feet, there's a wide smear of white disfiguring the left arm of his all-black kit and he's holding his jaw, shaking his head, dazed. Play resumes and England strive to exploit Tilkowski's discomfort. Peters gets off a sharp shot, but the keeper dives to tilt it away for England's first corner. Maybe he is rocky with the high balls, but he's agile and he's brave. Ball takes the kick. It falls to Hurst at an awkward height. He lets fly, but it's skewed. Crisis over. Tilkowski survives. West Germany exhales.

Ten minutes. Play is swaying from end to end. Beckenbauer, slim and upright, lifts a free kick towards Seeler, but Jack Charlton reads it, heads it, clears it. Brother Bobby, flowing, picks it up and lays it to Ball, scampering. Ball, looking even more boyish in his red England shirt than he's done in the white, snipes deep down the left. Schnellinger hastens over, but Ball swerves away from him. Schnellinger follows, a class act hell-bent on proving it, but Ball passes smartly, laterally, and Peters, down the right, checks back and gets it under control. It's he and Stiles who are finding the early space, a tribute to the efforts of the rest in displacing those who are policing them. Peters shoots, low. It's two feet wide. But England are edging the opening minutes.

At the other end, Held and Seeler have been probing, but apart from Held's heart-stopping opening right at the start, they've had no change so far. The England defenders don't religiously mark assigned players in open play, they mark space, covering it and endlessly pulling each other into the right configuration. Seeler, facing his own goal forty yards out, accepts a pass. Being an escape route for defenders is part of his job, the selfless part. Wilson, wired up, dives into a tackle, fouls, and dashes back to patrol his sector of the penalty area as West Germany take the kick and swing the ball out to Held on the left.

He's got Cohen in front of him. Not a happy sight for a forward twenty yards out and stationary. You can't barge past Cohen because he's hard as nails. You can't run past him, because he's like greased lightning. Held, constrained just as Cohen would wish, takes the only available option. He turns away and sends in a hopeful centre with his right foot. This is the kind of approach play defenders like best. They're facing the right way, there's no pace on the ball, it'll probably float out of touch. The best the strikers can hope for is a fluff. The ball wafts towards the head of Ray Wilson. He's thirty-one, an able, educated footballer with a generous, ebullient nature. He eats limp crosses like these for breakfast. He heads it. It goes nowhere. Not high and far away, not wide towards the corner flag. Just faintheartedly downwards towards the lurking figure of Helmut Haller.

Haller's got a barrel chest and a blond quiff and England think he doesn't care to mix it, but he's so assured. Stretching, he executes a half-trap that's just enough. Now, all the angles favour West Germany as the England defenders stand, stunned. Haller takes a long stride, places his left foot beside the ball and swings with his right. He doesn't really catch it right, but it rolls towards the goal at cruising speed. Jack Charlton shifts his weight to his left, but doesn't swing his foot. Banks shifts his weight to the right, but doesn't dive until it's too late. Haller's shot zips between them, crosses the line, and the author of England's sudden misery is ten feet tall and growing. It's England's first really costly defensive error of the entire tournament. Wilson slaps his hands on his knees and looks up at Jack Charlton, who is staring at Banks. It was a piddling little goal, a mess. Any one of the three of them might have prevented it. Nobody speaks, not even Big Jack. Nothing to do but get on with it.

Thirteen minutes. Haller, out on the right, slips past Stiles, who fouls him. Stiles argues with the referee, doing his up-down arm bit. Get on with it. Wilson is talking to himself: it's happened, it's over, get on with it. England are frantic to equalize: get on with it.

Seventeen minutes. Stiles heads to Bobby Charlton, who's playing well, making almost every touch count, although he's got nothing like the liberty he enjoyed against France and Portugal. Beckenbauer's always there. Charlton can't get by him, but he evades him, moving infield. He passes square to Moore, breaking from the back. Moore looks up. Overath faces him. Moore can't go past people from a standing start, any more than Held could have gone past Cohen prior to

Haller's goal. He swivels anti-clockwise, looking for an escape route. Overath snaps at his heels and Dienst blows for a foul.

As the West Germans get organized, Moore addresses the ball. The quick free kick, taken before the opposition is ready, has become *de rigueur*. Moore, with those little steps, starts to run up, stops, starts again and chips it directly towards the space in front of Tilkowski. Towards no one. Until Hurst arrives, in mid-air. He nods the ball into the bottom of the net and it just lies there, quietly. In the second it takes to create the goal, no one except he and Moore appear to have been actually playing. Tilkowski just stands there and points at the hole Hurst has filled so devastatingly. Höttges is yards away. Neither of these men has ever been to Chadwell Heath. One–all.

Twenty-two minutes. The sun comes out and the game opens up. There have been fewer goals scored per match in this World Cup so far than in any other, but one to each side in the first quarter of the final reduces inhibitions. The West Germans are angry with themselves for letting their lead slip. The English are thrilled and – Wilson in particular – relieved at restoring the equilibrium so quickly. Both goals have had impurities – Haller's has come from a mistake, Hurst's from a free kick which some refs would not have given – but the evidence of fallibility freshens the spectacle. And as the two teams exchange thrusts and parries, there is a feeling that anything could happen, any time, right out of the blue.

And both sides want to win. Just as there is stern

191

defence, so there is scope to attack. With the spirit willing on both sides, talent has room to bloom. Bobby Charlton, swerving away from Beckenbauer, has Tilkowski plunging at the foot of a post. Cohen, crab-like with his jutting elbows and busy feet, lofts a far-post cross to Hurst – such a complete modern centre-forward – who gets above everyone, heads down and sees Tilkowski save again, right on his line.

Seeler and Held are still stealing about, making England think. Peters gets booked, for no very obvious reason. The crowd chants: 'Oh, oh, what a referee!' Emmerich nearly goes clear, but Moore makes a sublime sliding tackle to rob him. The momentum stays with the home team. Bobby Charlton finds Hunt, fleetingly free of Weber, at the far post. A fierce, rising shot is parried by Tilkowski. But here's Seeler, suddenly loose, twenty-five yards out. He's in exactly the same position as when he administered the *coup de grâce* to Uruguay. He hits the same shot, with the same power, towards the same top corner of the goal that Mazurkieviez could not reach. But Banks does reach it. With a fingertip. The first half ends with Jack Charlton tearing upfield, shouting for a header. It's been an engrossing first forty-five. And there's very little in it.

Half-time, and Ramsey is calm. There are no new instructions to give, nothing unusual to say. You're doing all right, but you could do better. Concentrate. Work for it. It'll come.

Over Wembley, the heavens open. The players resume soaked to the skin. There's a spot more sparring and some fraying tempers. Big Jack goes rigid with rage

192

at Mr Dienst after a cock-up over a corner. Stiles is whistled for a foul, and bounces the ball on the ground in anger. The pitch starts cutting up and play becomes bogged down. On the left Wilson and Moore are polished, down the right Cohen and Ball are relentless, but it all comes down to long, airy crosses, and Schulz and company cope comfortably. Beckenbauer fluffs a shooting chance, and the West German front three look neutered. The crowd again sing, 'What a referee,' but this time it's just for fun.

Everywhere it's trench warfare. Ball starts running everywhere, determined to wipe Schnellinger out. Haller comes deeper and deeper. Stiles fouls him, Haller rolls over, Stiles leans over him, waving his arms, yelling, get up, come on, get up. Ball calms him, Haller rises, handshakes all round, then it's back to barking at the defence. Tilkowski gets injured again. Bobby Charlton shoots over by inches. The players are kicking up mud at the West German end. And suddenly it's the West Germans who are looking the more tired.

Seventy-three minutes. Ball catches Schnellinger in possession and releases Hunt on a counter-attack. Hunt almost puts Hurst in for a shot, but Tilkowski fields. England stay on the offensive. Ball has a shot saved for a corner and jogs over to take it himself. He floats it across. Jack Charlton and Peters jump, nobody connects. Legs look heavy, the ball looks heavy. It comes to Hurst, who glances up. He's got little to aim at, but he still tries a shot. Rolling towards Höttges it looks harmless, one for Tilkowski just to pick up. But Höttges takes a swipe, slips and the ball flips freakishly upwards and across his own goal-face. Hearts stop. Jack Charlton, Hunt and Peters know precisely what's coming towards them. It's a gift. Who's going to accept it? Peters does. Seventy-eight minutes. Two–one.

Everyone struggles to adjust, England to their excitement, West Germany to their despair. There is no clock to consult, but the players know they are going into the last ten minutes. There are signals from the bench, but their own internal hour-glasses are telling them, and the crowd, too, is like one vast, engulfing, living timepiece. It reacts to entering the last lap of the match, not with nervous quiet, but with an almost unaccountable confidence. Jack Charlton, as if to scoff at Corinthian niceties, considers his options twenty yards from his own goal, turns, dribbles the ball backwards and passes it to Banks. This diligently uneventful manoeuvre takes up maybe fifteen seconds. That's one quarter of one of what is now about nine minutes to go. Tick, tick, edging nearer. But the crowd require heroics. Up goes the Shout: 'WE WANT THREE! WE WANT THREE!' Tempting fate with gay abandon, they want glory, England's glory.

But what a bonus three would be. Almost all the agony of the, what, the eight and a half minutes left would be drained away. Ball's in possession out on the right and looking about, as if sniffing the air for the scent of a clincher. Hunt comes steaming in to his line of vision. Ball produces one of his bespoke short passes and Hunt, taking it in his stride, eases the ball further left to the spindly Peters. He's got twenty yards to go and time to look up as the West Germans, unravelled, retreat. But the shot is frail, more of a scoop. It wafts over the bar, barely making the necessary distance. The pitch is scuffed and pitted. Peters stands weakly amid the mud.

Seven minutes left and the crowd breaks into 'Rule, Britannia!'. Of the West Germans only Held looks less than kaput. He's badgering forward, now, twenty-five yards out, gets half past a wholly dishevelled Stiles, who leans into him, shoulders and elbows, frantic to get the ball back. Mr Dienst blows for a foul and Stiles is, as ever, possessed with the injustice of it, arms waving all over the place. He's still organizing anyone within earshot when Emmerich floats the free kick over the England wall and there's Weber up from the back, an almost lonesome figure eight yards out, and the ball skims off his forehead and away, harmlessly for a goal-kick, as Banks goes absolutely crackers.

Six minutes left. 'Rule, Britannia' has faded now, and all that remains are nerves, crucifying nerves. On the edge of the centre-circle Moore challenges Schnellinger for a bouncing ball, going in with his foot high, his leg parallel with the ground. Rarely does Moore look so rushed or risk a tackle so injudicious. The free kick goes nowhere much, but the ball wends wearily for a West German corner, then comes to Moore again. He's down by the other corner-flag and hemmed in. But this time we see the authentic Moore. Shoulders hunched, elbows out, blond, assured. Others would just whack it, but Moore bisects the harrying West Germans with a ten-yard pass to Peters. Impossibly, Peters hears a shout from Ball, still running. Then Ball, in a moment of brilliant vision, strikes a superb reverse-angle pass to Hunt. He is suddenly, thrillingly in the clear.

Five minutes left. It's Hunt bombing upfield with just one West German in front of him and the rest trailing. He can't make it alone and pokes a pass with the outside of his right boot for Bobby Charlton to run on to, but it's a fraction under strength and Charlton can't quite get there. It isn't finished yet.

One minute left. Banks takes a goal-kick. It lands near halfway and there's a few seconds of heading tennis. Untidy stuff. The ball ends up back near England's penalty area, towards Jack Charlton and Held. They both jump. The ball is nearer Held, whose back faces the England goal, but Charlton is much the bigger man. These are the last, half-crazed seconds. Held strains for it, Charlton arches upwards and for-wards, looming over the West German. He gets his head to the ball, but neat Mr Dienst gives a foul. It's just one of those messy tussles. Did Charlton push or Held obstruct?

Big Jack would quite like an argument, but this isn't the time for it. It's time for England to build a wall, their final wall. Peters is in it, and Bobby Charlton. Stiles is marshalling, utterly bedraggled, tugging at his team mates as if he's on the brink of some kind of breakdown. Emmerich takes the kick. He lofts the ball over the wall and the heads of the three Englishmen turn. There's a ruck, a muddle. Cohen's in there, so's Schnellinger, and the ball pops up and hits him on the back. There's Seeler, Moore, Wilson on the line. There's the ball, bouncing loose, and there's Weber sliding in with a long right leg . . .

Weber equalizes.

No minutes left. England have barely kicked off when Herr Dienst blows the final whistle. West Germany have scrambled from the grave and into extra time.

Jimmy Armfield, as unofficial captain of the second team, has been asked by Ramsey to lead the reserves down from their stand seats via the lift behind the royal box and out through the tunnel beneath to join him by the bench just before the end. They can't keep back the disappointment of not being involved, even those who knew they wouldn't be, but they are still thrilled to have a part in the showpiece. As Armfield leads the way back into daylight, however, he sees the free kick, watches the men in the wall spin round, sees the great muddle of knees and shoulders, Weber's swoop and his bounce of delight. Some of the others miss it. They just hear the crowd and think that must be it, Mr Dienst has ended the agony. But then a few of them catch a glimpse of Ramsey's face, and catch a private second of distress. But then he turns to get on with his job; his mask of impassivity has been put back into place.

He doesn't rush on to the pitch, just walks with a sense of purpose towards his exhausted team. In disbelief they huddle around him as Shepherdson and Cocker sponge faces and massage screaming calves. Moore sits on the grass, Bobby Charlton looks half-drowned in his own sweat. Ball, standing slightly apart, angrily slings his tie-ups. They suck oranges and listen.

These are shocked, fleeting moments and heads are bowed as Ramsey speaks. He has a simple message for his players. With concentrated calmness he observes that they have already beaten the other team once. All they need to do now is go out and beat them again. He indicates the West German players being exhorted by Schoen. He tells the England players just to look at them, look at that lot, they are finished. Banks hears Stiles say: 'We can fuck them.'

Ball thinks they can too. He's already putting the ball down on the centre-spot, ready to go again. Meanwhile, up in the crowd, his dad is having to drag himself away. He's just got a job with Stoke City and he's been watching with a bunch of his new colleagues, including Tony Waddington, the team manager. They have a flight to catch to Dublin and hadn't banked on extra-time. Ball's dad can't bear to leave. His lad is playing a blinder. But Waddington says: 'We're going.'

Ball junior is going as well. Going and going and going, like he's been sponsored by Ever Ready. He hits a swerving shot which Tilkowski tips over. Schnellinger goes down, limping. England, incredibly, have the most fuel left in the tank. Bobby Charlton hits a post. Then Stiles gets possession. They say Stiles can't actually play the game of football. Well, he plays it all right at this moment. It's a crafted pass, arcing over the head of Schnellinger of Milan, leaving him ragged, and if Ball of Blackpool had a pocket in his shorts it would have landed straight in it. Instead, it just hits the ground, rolls and slows, coming almost to a halt as Ball runs on to it, managing the nearest thing to a sprint that any of the twenty outfield players can muster.

As Höttges throws himself across to cover, Ball crosses. It isn't quite perfect. Hurst has to check and twist his body back against his own momentum, and get his right foot up high to cushion the bouncing ball somehow back down to the ground. He's close to goal, but all the angles are against him. Striving to improve them, he chops his stride, and, falling away, shoots on the half-volley. The hardest thing from such a position is to keep the ball down. Hurst does pretty well. The ball slaps against the underside of the crossbar right above Tilkowski's head, rebounds hard down to the ground, then bounces, spinning, back into play.

Hunt is following up. He turns and jumps for joy. Goal! Is it? Mr Dienst hesitates. Everyone stares in his direction. Oh, what a referee. Play halts and gives way to mass appealing. Ball, Hurst, Hunt and Bobby Charlton cry, Yes, goal! Weber, Tilkowski, Höttges, implore, No goal! Dienst runs towards the touchline, where Tofik Bakhramov waits. With 93,000 people howling in their ears, the Swiss referee and the Azerbaijani linesman confer. Can they hear each other speak? They stand close together, barking, their heads wagging earnestly. Ball and Hunt eavesdrop. They hear Bakhramov say, 'Goal!' and Dienst points towards the centre-spot.

Goal!

Pandemonium. Bakhramov is besieged by Germans, but he's used to that: in the last war he fought for his country on the Eastern front. Seeler shepherds his team mates away. The England supporters go crazy. Again, they cry for the kill. They chant: 'WE WANT FOUR! WE WANT FOUR!'

The whistle goes for the end of the first half of extra time. A few players totter towards the benches to be patched up and absorb a few more words of managerial advice. Socks are down, shirts are stained, hair is drenched. Cramp eats into calf muscles. England are exhausted, but they want this business finished. They've been away from their homes for too long. They need a replay on Wednesday night like a hole in the head.

England attack. Ball goes pelting down the left and, amazingly, incredibly, finds Wilson overlapping with a back-heel trick pass that he'd have got shot for if it had gone astray. But Ball is flying. The sun is shining. The crowd is whistling and chanting: 'ENG-LAND! ENG-LAND!'

How long now? Ten minutes? Five minutes? It's just a long, agonizing blur. Both teams keep trying to score. Hurst shoots wide and hobbles away. Held is still running, he's on the edge of the penalty area and in slides Hunt to deny him. Two minutes? Schulz comes forward. He swings in a long, deep cross. Haller goes up, heads it down, but it skids away from Seeler. The West German chases, saves the goal-kick, turns, passes back to Schulz, who hits another long, deep cross. Cohen heads it away for a corner.

One minute? Haller takes the corner. It's cleared. Here's Schulz yet again, crossing long and deep yet again. Moore intercepts. He takes it on his chest, so immaculate, not a crease in his bootlaces, and shepherds the ball towards the corner-flag. He exchanges passes with Ball then looks up. Jack Charlton's screaming at him to clear it, hoof it anywhere, get rid of it, but Moore keeps looking up. Then some little steps forward and a precise swing of his left leg . . .

Then it's with Hurst, near the centre-circle, getting it under control, looking as if he has hardly the strength to drag himself along. But nor do the West Germans. He heads off downfield, not sure quite where, somewhere in the direction of the goal. Right foot, right foot, right foot, coming to the edge of the box, across the ragged turf. The ball begins to bobble, and Hurst tilts slightly away to his left. He's thinking where to go. Turn away, hold it, waste a few seconds more? To his right he hears Ball, still with enough breath to bellow after running the length of the pitch. He's all alone, he's shouting for a pass.

Hurst thinks: hit it, hard and high. If it's over the bar, it's over the stand as well. Overath is upon him. Hurst draws back his left foot. 'You bastard!' shrieks Ball, the last syllable leaving his mouth as Hurst's shot hurtles towards its target, past Tilkowski as if he isn't there, and screams into the net. 'Great shot!' whoops Ball, and he leaps on Hurst, who turns with his arm raised in salute.

Four–two. Herr Dienst sounds three long peeps on his whistle, the West Germans' chins drop on to their chests, Big Jack Charlton falls to his knees with his face in his hands and his brother Bobby bursts into tears. Everyone else embraces. The reserves rush on to the field, Greaves has a hug for Nobby Stiles and for Bobby

Moore, his friend. Shepherdson, Cocker and Bass rush on as well and so, very shortly, will the other man sitting with them. But just for a couple of moments, while the rest of the country goes wild, Alf Ramsey, Englishman and professional, stays quietly on his seat.

Post-Match

THE SIGHTS and sounds that followed Geoff Hurst's third goal have remained wedged in the minds of millions. They survive as slivers of collective memory, as raw material for media folk, even as triggers for moral parables about the state of the nation. British Telecom used a shot of Bobby Moore chaired by his team mates and holding the Jules Rimet trophy aloft in its 1995 '1 to Remember' campaign. Kenneth Wolstenholme's few seconds of priceless commentary which accompanied the clinching strike – for the record: 'Some people are on the pitch . . . they think it's all over . . . it is now' – provide the title and sign-off line for a risqué television quiz show. My favourite bit of World Cup mental memorabilia is when Bobby Moore wipes his hands on his shorts, shirt and the side of the royal box before receiving the cup from the Queen.

Moore's later explanation for this was prosaic: he was worried about soiling Her Majesty's white gloves. But some now see in his gesture decisive evidence of a finer era long demolished, a kind of Wembley Stadium of the national spirit, with chivalry and deference as its twin towers, with the monarch as its blameless guardian and Moore representing the dauntless decency of the English working class. Moore was certainly eulogized in much these terms when, so sadly, he died in 1993. Add Nobby Stiles doing his wacky lap-of-honour war-dance and perhaps a Spitfire doing a victory roll overhead, and you have enough raw material to keep romantic patriots in reveries for years.

I must admit, though, that it's a seductive tableau and we all take our own meanings from it. To me 1966 has long seemed a great year, one from the decade's innocent middle period, full of excitement, optimism, Tamla Motown and all the sex you could eat. Shame I was only eight at the time. It all sustains an illusion of lost national well-being which defies the economic and political facts of the time. Harold Wilson, of course, understood perfectly, as shown by his intervention in the scene on the balcony of the Royal Garden Hotel. Lord Harewood encouraged him, but the late Harold didn't take much pushing to join Alf Ramsey, his staff and his squad as they waved at the happy throng in Kensington High Street below. He might have stayed all night if Denis Howell hadn't suggested that maybe enough was enough.

It must have been quite a night. George Brown, heartily plastered, sang 'I'm forever blowing bubbles' and David Corbett turned up with Pickles, demanding, successfully, to be let in (Pickles died tragically some weeks later, accidentally strangled with his own leash). Some of the players, though, were quite keen to escape. Martin Peters slipped away to be with his wife, Alan Ball did the same with his fiancée. Jimmy Greaves slipped away and got very miserably drunk. Jack Charlton got very happily drunk and woke up in a garden in Walthamstow, or was it a front room in Leytonstone, or on a patio in Whipps Cross?

In later years they again went in various directions. Some, as is well known, have remained in football, while others just watch the odd game on TV. Bobby Charlton, Bobby Moore, Geoff Hurst, Nobby Stiles and Martin Peters all tried club management, but not for long. Some have found other roles in football, as did Gordon Banks, who lost an eye in a car crash in 1973. Alan Ball, typically, persevered with management. Jack Charlton had his ups and downs in the same dangerous occupation and eventually became an Irish saint. Roger Hunt went into the family haulage business, but later worked for the pools panel. Others walked away from football altogether. Ray Wilson went into the family funeral-direction business. George Cohen struggled against illness and survived to make his living in property. John Connelly runs a fish and chip restaurant where I intend to eat one day. Hurst and Peters converted to insurance. Jimmy Greaves became an alcoholic, then a television personality. He is the only member of the World Cup squad who's played no part in the squad's occasional reunions.

But the striking thing about these men is their loyalty to each other and Alf Ramsey. Those who might have argued that they deserved a bigger share insisted that the £22,000 winners' bonus be split equally among the squad as a whole. Today not one of them, Greaves included, has a bad word to say about any of the others in public, despite the fact that, these days, they might earn plenty of money from doing so. Ramsey himself lives in quiet retirement in Ipswich. He led England to Mexico to defend the World Cup in 1970, but his team was dramatically eliminated in the quarter-final by West Germany. The cup was duly claimed by a revitalized Pele and the rest of the 'boys from Brazil'. After failing to qualify for the 1974 tournament he was sacked by the FA and was never wholehearted about football management again.

Ramsey was knighted after the World Cup victory, and Moore got an OBE. Bobby Charlton was also awarded an OBE following Manchester United's European Cup win in 1968 (beating Benfica and poor Eusebio) and has recently been knighted as well. His brother has an OBE too. Otherwise, though, the 'boys of '66' remain conspicuously unennobled. Indeed there has been little formal recognition of their achievement. The silver jubilee of their victory was not marked by the Football Association, and in researching this book I have heard more than one poignant tale of a frail elderly gentleman sitting alone on the fringes of England international post-match receptions with nobody to talk to. That man is Alf Ramsey, the only England manager who's ever won anything.

But while monuments and gongs serve their purpose, when it comes to appreciation there is no substitute for the special acknowledgement that comes only from being enshrined in public affection. This is what happened to Banks, Cohen, Wilson, Stiles, Charlton J., Moore (captain), Ball, Hunt, Charlton R., Hurst and

Peters, Alf Ramsey and all. Unlike too many modern sportsmen, they are famous for what they achieved, and achieved together, rather than just being famous for being well known.

Thanks

THIS ACCOUNT has been compiled from numerous books, old newspapers and bits of film and television footage, and, most importantly, from the memories, insights and imaginations of various people (including myself) who played different parts in the drama of the 1966 World Cup, whether as players, broadcasters, organizers, or spectators. My sincere thanks to the following for their time: David Barber; Graham Smith; Roger Hunt; John Williams; Alan Ball; Rogan Taylor; David Coleman; Norman Hunter; Denis Howell; Jimmy Armfield; John Connelly; Ray Wilson; Bryan Cowgill; Alec Weeks; Peter Dimmock; David Meek; Eric Paylor; John Wilson; Sheila Spiers; Joe Stanton.

The following books, many of them now out of print, provided factual detail, insights into characters and reminders of sights, sounds and feelings of excitement that I had never quite forgotten. My special thanks to John Duncan of the *Guardian* for allowing me to borrow from his collection and to David Barber at the FA for the loan of the *World Cup Report* and the *Official Handbook*.

Armfield, Jim: *Fighting Back* (The Soccer Book Club, 1963)

Ball, Alan: *It's About a Ball* (W. H. Allen, 1978)

Banks, Gordon: *Banks of England* (Sportsmedia, 1980)

Eusebio: *My Name is Eusebio* (Routledge & Kegan Paul, 1967)

Glanville, Brian: *The Story of the World Cup* (Faber & Faber, 1993)

Greaves, Jimmy, and Giller, Norman: *Don't Shoot the Manager* (Boxtree, 1994)

Hopcraft, Arthur: *The Football Man* (Sportspages, 1990)

Hunt, Roger: *Hunt for Goals* (Pelham, 1969)

Hutchinson, Roger: *It Is Now* (Mainstream Publishing, 1995)

Marquis, Max: *Sir Alf Ramsey – Anatomy of a Football Manager* (Arthur Barker, 1970)

Mayes, Harold: *World Cup Report, 1966* (William Heinemann, 1967)

Moore, Bobby: *England! England!* (Stanley Paul, 1970)

Paylor, Eric and Wilson, John: *Ayresome Park Memories* (Breedon Books, 1995)

Rogan, Johnny: *The Football Managers* (Macdonald/Queen Anne Press, 1989)

Smith, Leslie: *Harold Wilson* (Fontana, 1964)

Stiles, Nobby: *Soccer, My Battlefield* (Corgi, 1969)

Taylor, Rogan and Ward, Andrew: *Kicking and Screaming – An Oral History of Football in England* (Robson Books, 1995)

THANKS

Wagg, Stephen: *The Football World* (Harvester Press, 1984)

Wilson, Ray: *My Life in Soccer* (Pelham, 1969)

World Championship Official Handbook 1966

Thanks also to Andy Lyons of *When Saturday Comes*, David Sadler for contacts, Phil Crossley of the BFI for running a copy of the movie *Goal!*, to the London office of the *New Yorker* magazine, to George Morley, to Sara Fisher, to the divine Sheila Fitzsimons and to Carmel, Moira and Pat for helping Sheila put up with Absent Man Syndrome.

Facts

Group One

England 0 Uruguay 0 (Monday, 11 July, Wembley)
France 1 Mexico 1 (Wednesday, 13 July, Wembley)
Uruguay 2 France 1 (Friday, 15 July, White City)
England 2 Mexico 0 (Saturday, 16 July, Wembley)
Uruguay 0 Mexico 0 (Tuesday, 19 July, Wembley)
England 2 France 0 (Wednesday, 20 July, Wembley)

FINAL TABLE

	P	W	D	L	F	A	Pts
England	3	2	1	0	4	0	5
Uruguay	3	1	2	0	2	1	4
Mexico	3	0	2	1	1	3	2
France	3	0	1	2	2	5	1

Group Two

West Germany 5 Switzerland 0 (Tuesday, 12 July, Hillsborough)
Argentina 2 Spain 1 (Wednesday, 13 July, Villa Park)
Spain 2 Switzerland 1 (Friday, 15 July, Hillsborough)

Argentina 0 West Germany 0 (Saturday, 16 July, Villa
   Park)
Argentina 2 Switzerland 0 (Tuesday, 19 July,
   Hillsborough)
West Germany 2 Spain 1 (Wednesday, 20 July, Villa
   Park)

FINAL TABLE

	P	W	D	L	F	A	Pts
West Germany	3	2	1	0	7	1	5
Argentina	3	2	1	0	4	1	5
Spain	3	1	0	2	4	5	2
Switzerland	3	0	0	3	1	9	0

Group Three

Brazil 2 Bulgaria 0 (Tuesday, 12 July, Goodison Park)
Portugal 3 Hungary 1 (Wednesday, 13 July, Old
   Trafford)
Hungary 3 Brazil 1 (Friday, 15 July, Goodison Park)
Portugal 3 Bulgaria 0 (Saturday, 16 July, Old Trafford)
Portugal 3 Brazil 1 (Tuesday, 19 July, Goodison Park)
Hungary 3 Bulgaria 1 (Wednesday, 20 July, Old
   Trafford)

FINAL TABLE

	P	W	D	L	F	A	Pts
Portugal	3	3	0	0	9	2	6
Hungary	3	2	0	1	7	5	4
Brazil	3	1	0	2	4	6	2
Bulgaria	3	0	0	3	1	8	0

Group Four

USSR 3 North Korea 0 (Tuesday, 12 July, Ayresome Park)

Italy 2 Chile 0 (Wednesday, 13 July, Roker Park)

North Korea 1 Chile 1 (Friday, 15 July, Ayresome Park)

Italy 0 USSR 1 (Saturday, 16 July, Roker Park)

Italy 0 North Korea 1 (Tuesday, 19 July, Ayresome Park)

Chile 1 USSR 2 (Wednesday, 20 July, Roker Park)

FINAL TABLE

	P	W	D	L	F	A	Pts
USSR	3	3	0	0	6	1	6
North Korea	3	1	1	1	2	4	3
Italy	3	1	0	2	2	2	2
Chile	3	0	1	2	2	5	1

Quarter-Finals

England 1 Argentina 0 (Saturday, 23 July, Wembley)
West Germany 4 Uruguay 0 (Saturday, 23 July, Hillsborough)
Portugal 5 North Korea 3 (Saturday, 23 July, Goodison Park)
USSR 2 Hungary 1 (Saturday, 23 July, Roker Park)

Semi-Finals

West Germany 2 USSR 1 (Monday, 25 July, Goodison Park)
England 2 Portugal 1 (Tuesday, 26 July, Wembley)

Third and Fourth Place Final

Portugal 2 USSR 1 (Thursday, 28 July, Wembley)

Final

England 4 West Germany 2 (Saturday, 30 July, Wembley)
(after extra time)